"COME, YE CHILDREN."

A BOOK FOR
PARENTS AND TEACHERS
ON THE

CHRISTIAN TRAINING OF CHILDREN.

BY

C. H. SPUR[...]

*" Come, ye children, hearken unto me; [...]
of the Lord."*—Psalm x[...]

Publishers of Spurgeon's *Metropolitan Tabernacle Pulpit*
sermon series and other Spurgeon "originals."

Catalog sent free on request.

 Pilgrim PUBLICATIONS, Pasadena, Texas 77501

SETS BY CHARLES HADDON SPURGEON

Pilgrim Publications is the only source for exact reprints of sets by C. H. Spurgeon which were originally published by Spurgeon's London publisher, Passmore & Alabaster, in the last century.

• **THE NEW PARK STREET PULPIT** consists of the first six volumes of the Spurgeon sermon series, covering the years 1855-1860, sermons #1-347. Our edition is in three large double-volumes, two years to each book.

• **THE METROPOLITAN TABERNACLE PULPIT** consists of volume 7 thru volume 63 of the Spurgeon sermon series, covering years 1861 thru 1917, sermons #348-3561.

• **THE TREASURY OF DAVID** is the seven-volume commentary on the Book of Psalms, twenty years in the making and the most extensive work ever accomplished on this book.

The Pilgrim reprints are all unedited, unabridged, and reproduced directly from the Passmore & Alabaster original sets. All the reprints are bound in durable cloth bindings, stamped in gold. We have cut no corners in providing this generation with reprint editions of quality and enduring value.

Our books are usually available from Christian Book Stores; if there is no store in your area, feel free to write directly to **Pilgrim Publications, Box 66, Pasadena, Texas 77501.**

CONTENTS.

———◆———

C. H. SPURGEON AND A GROUP OF ORPHAN BOYS.

"FEED MY LAMBS"—HOW TO DO IT.

THE best of the church are none too good for this work. Do not think because you have other service to do that therefore you should take no interest in this form of holy work, but kindly, according to your opportunities, stand ready to help the little ones, and to cheer those whose chief calling is to attend to them. To us all this message comes : " Feed My lambs." To the minister, and to all who have any knowledge of the things of God, the commission is given. See to it that you look after the children that are in Christ Jesus. Peter was a leader among believers, yet he must feed the lambs.

The lambs are the young of the flock. So, then, we ought to look specially and carefully after those who are young in grace. They may be old in years, and yet they may be mere babes in grace as to the length of their spiritual life, and therefore they need to be under a good shepherd. As soon as a person is converted and added to the church, he should become the object of the care and kindness of his fellow-members. He has but newly come among us, and has no familiar friends among the saints, therefore let us all be friendly to him. Even should we leave our older comrades, we must be doubly kind towards those who are newly escaped from the world, and have come to find a refuge with the Almighty and His people. Watch with ceaseless care over those new-born babes who are strong in desires, but strong in nothing else. They have but just crept out of darkness, and their eyes can scarcely bear the light; let us be a shade to them until they grow accustomed to the blaze of gospel day. Addict yourselves to the holy work of caring for the feeble and despondent. Peter himself that morning must have felt like a newly-enlisted soldier, for he had in a sense ended his public Christian life by denying his Lord, and he had begun it again when he "went out and wept bitterly." He was now making a new confession of his faith before his Lord and his brethren, and, therefore, because he was thus made to sympathise with recruits he is commissioned to act as a guardian to them. Young converts are too timid to ask our help, and so our Lord introduces them to us, and with an emphatic word of command He says, "Feed My lambs." This shall be our reward: "Inasmuch as ye have done it unto one of the least of these, ye have done it unto Me."

However young a believer may be, he should make an open confession of his faith, and be folded with the rest of the flock of Christ. We are not among those who are suspicious of youthful piety : we could never see more reason for such suspicions in the case of the young than in the case of those who repent late in life. Of the two we think the latter are more to be questioned than the former : for a selfish fear of punishment and dread of death are more likely to produce a counterfeit faith than mere childishness would be. How much has the child missed which might have spoiled it ! How much it does not know which, please God, we hope it never may know ! Oh, how much there is of brightness and trustfulness about children when converted to God which is not seen in elder converts ! Our Lord Jesus evidently felt deep sympathy with children, and he is but little like Christ who looks upon them as a trouble in the world, and treats them as if they must needs be either little deceivers or foolish simpletons. To you who teach in our schools is given this joyous privilege of finding out where these young disciples are who are truly the lambs of Christ's flock, and to you He saith, " Feed My lambs " ; that is, instruct such as are truly gracious, but young in years.

It is very remarkable that the word used here for " feed My lambs " is very different from the word employed in the precept, " feed My sheep." I will not trouble you with Greek words, but the second " feed " means exercise the office of a shepherd, rule, regulate, lead, manage them, do all that a shepherd has to do towards a flock ; but this first feed does not include all that : it means distinctly *feed*, and it directs teachers to a duty which they may, perhaps, neglect—namely, that of instructing children in the faith. The lambs do not so much need keeping in order as we do who know so much, and yet know so little : who think we are so far advanced that we judge one another, and contend and emulate. Christian children mainly need to be taught the doctrine, precept, and life of the gospel : they require to have Divine truth put before them clearly and forcibly. Why should the higher doctrines, the doctrines of grace, be kept back from them ? They are not as some say, bones ; or if they be bones, they are full of marrow, and covered with fatness. If there be any doctrine too difficult for a child, it is rather the fault of the teacher's conception of it than of the child's power to receive it, provided that child be really converted to God. It is ours to make doctrine simple ; this is to be a main part of our work. Teach the little ones the whole truth and nothing but the truth ; for instruction is the great want of the child's nature. A child has not only to live as you and I have, but also to grow ; hence he has double need of food. When fathers say of their boys, " What appetites they have ! " they should remember that we also would have great appetites if we had not only to keep the machinery going, but to enlarge it at the same time. Children in grace have to grow, rising to greater capacity in knowing, being, doing, and feeling, and to greater power from God ; therefore above all things they must be fed. They must be well fed or instructed, because they are in danger of having their cravings perversely satisfied with error. Youth is susceptible to evil doctrine. Whether *we* teach young Christians truth or not, the devil will be sure to teach them error. They will hear of it somehow, even if they are watched by the most careful guardians. The only way to keep chaff out of the child's little measure is to fill it brimful with good wheat. Oh, that the Spirit of God may help us to do this ! The more the young are taught the better ; it will keep them from being misled.

We are specially exhorted to feed them because they are so likely to be overlooked. I am afraid our sermons often go over the heads of the younger folk—who, nevertheless, may be as true Christians as the older ones. Blessed is he who can so speak as to be understood by a child ! Blessed is that godly woman who in her class so adapts herself to girlish modes of thought that the truth from her heart streams into the children's hearts without let or hindrance.

We are specially exhorted to feed the young because this work is so profitable. Do what we may with persons converted late in life, we can never make much of them. We are very glad of them for their own sakes ; but at seventy what remains even if they live another ten years ? Train up a child, and he may have fifty years of holy service before him. We are glad to welcome those who come into the vineyard at the eleventh hour, but they have hardly taken their pruning-hook and their spade before the sun goes down, and their short day's work is ended. The time spent in training the late convert is greater than the space reserved for his actual service : but you take a child-convert and teach him well, and as early piety often becomes eminent piety, and that eminent piety may have a stretch of years before it in which God may be glorified and others may be blessed, such work is profitable in a high degree. It is also most beneficial work to ourselves. It exercises our humility and helps to keep us lowly and meek. It also trains our patience ; let those who doubt this try it ; for even young Christians exercise the patience of those who believe in them, and are therefore anxious that they should justify their confidence. If you want big-souled, large-hearted men or women, look for them among those who are much engaged among the young, bearing with their follies, and sympathising with their weaknesses for Jesus' sake.

DO NOT HINDER THE CHILDREN.

CONCERNING this hindering of children, let us watch its action. I think the results of this sad feeling about children coming to the Saviour is to be seen, first, in the fact that often there is nothing in the service for the children. The sermon is over their heads, and the preacher does not think that this is any fault ; in fact, he rather rejoices that it is so. Some time ago a person who wanted, I suppose, to make me feel my own insignificance, wrote to say that he had met with a number of negroes who had read my sermons with evident pleasure ; and he wrote that he believed they were very suitable for niggers. Yes, my preaching was just the sort of stuff for niggers. The gentleman did not dream what sincere pleasure he caused me ; for if I am understood by poor people, by servant-girls, by children, I am sure I can be understood by others. I am ambitious of preaching for niggers, if by these you mean the lowest, the rag-tag and bob-tail. I think nothing greater than to win the hearts of the lowly. So with regard to children. People occasionally

say of such a one, " He is only fit to teach children :
he is no preacher." I tell you, in God's sight he is no
preacher who does not care for the children.   There
should be at least a part of every sermon and
service that will suit the little ones.   It is an error
which permits us to forget this.

Parents sin in the same way when they omit
religion from the education of their children.
Perhaps the thought is that their children cannot
be converted while they are children, and so they
think it of small consequence where they go to
school in their tender years.   But it is not so
Many parents even forget this when their girls and
boys are closing their school-days.   They send
them away to the Continent, to places foul with
every moral and spiritual danger, with the idea
that there they can complete an elegant education.
In how many cases I have seen that education
completed, and it has produced young men who
are thorough-paced profligates, and young women
who are mere flirts.   As we sow we reap.   Let us
expect our children to know the Lord.   Let us
from the beginning mingle the name of Jesus with
their A B C.   Let them read their first lessons
from the Bible.   It is a remarkable thing that there
is no book from which children learn to read so
quickly as from the New Testament : there is a
charm about that book which draws forth the infant
mind.   But let us never be guilty, as parents, of
forgetting the religious training of our children ;
for if we do we may be guilty of the blood of
their souls.

Another result is that the conversion of children is not expected in many of our churches and congregations. I mean, that they do not expect the children to be converted as children. The theory is that if we can impress youthful minds with principles which may, in after years, prove useful to them, we have done a great deal ; but to convert children as children, and to regard them as being as much believers as their seniors, is regarded as absurd. To this supposed absurdity I cling with all my heart. I believe that of children is the kingdom of God, both on earth and in heaven.

Another ill-result is that the conversion of children is not believed in. Certain suspicious people always file their teeth a bit when they hear of a newly-converted child : they will have a bite at him if they can. They very rightly insist upon it that these children should be carefully examined before they are baptized and admitted into the church ; but they are wrong in insisting that only in exceptional instances are they to be received. We quite agree with them as to the care to be exercised ; but it should be the same in all cases, and neither more nor less in the cases of children.

How often do people expect to see in boys and girls the same solemnity of behaviour which is seen in older people ! It would be a good thing for us all if we had never left off being boys and girls, but had added to all the excellencies of a child the virtues of a man. Surely it is not necessary to kill the child to make the saint ? It is thought by the more severe that a converted child must become twenty years older in a minute. A very solemn person once called me from the playground after I had joined the church and warned me of the impropriety of playing at trap, bat, and ball with the boys. He said, " How can you play like others, if you are a child of God ? " I answered that I was employed as an usher, and it was part of my duty to join in the amusements of the boys. My venerable critic thought that this altered the matter very materially ; but it was clearly his view that a converted boy, as such, ought never to play !

Do not others expect from children more perfect conduct than they themselves exhibit ? If a gracious child should lose his temper, or act wrongly in some trifling thing through forgetfulness, straightway he is condemned as a little hypocrite by those who are a long way from being perfect themselves. Jesus says, " Take heed that ye despise not one of these little ones." Take heed that ye say not an unkind word against your younger brethren in Christ, your little sisters in the Lord. Jesus sets such great store by His dear lambs, that He carries them in His bosom ; and I charge you who follow your Lord in all things to show a like tenderness to the little ones of the Divine family.

" They brought young children to Him, that He should touch them : and His disciples rebuked those that brought them. But when Jesus saw it He was much displeased." He was not often displeased ; certainly He was not often " much displeased," and when He was much displeased we may be sure that the case was serious. He was displeased at these children being pushed away from Him, for it was so contrary to His mind about them. The disciples did *wrong to the mothers ;* they rebuked the parents for doing a motherly act—for doing, in fact, that which Jesus loved them to do. They brought their children to Jesus out of respect to Him : they valued a blessing from His hands more than gold ; they expected that the benediction of God would go with the touch of the great Prophet. They may have hoped that a touch of the hand of Jesus would make their children's lives bright and happy. Though there may have been a measure of weakness in the parents' thought, yet the Saviour could not judge hardly of that which arose out of reverence to His person. He was therefore much displeased to think that those good women, who meant Him honour, should be roughly repulsed.

There was also wrong done to the children. Sweet little ones ! What had they done that they should be chided for coming to Jesus ? They had not meant to intrude. Dear things ! they would have fallen at His feet in reverent love for the sweet-voiced Teacher, who charmed not only men, but children, by His tender words. The little ones meant no ill, and why should they be blamed ?

Besides, there was wrong done to Himself. It might have made men think that Jesus was stiff, reserved, and self-exalted, like the Rabbins. If they had thought that He could not condescend to

children they would have sadly slandered the repute
of His great love. His heart was a great harbour
wherein many little ships might cast anchor. Jesus,
the child-man, was never more at home than with
children. The holy child Jesus had an affinity for
children. Was He to be represented by His own
disciples as shutting the door against the children?
It would do a sad injury to His character. Therefore, grieved at the triple evil which wounded the
mothers, the children, and Himself, He was sore
displeased. Anything we do to hinder a dear child
from coming to Jesus greatly displeases our dear
Lord. He cries to us, " Stand off. Let them
alone. Let them come to Me, and forbid them
not."

Next, it was contrary to His teaching; for He
went on to say, " Whosoever shall not receive the
kingdom of God as a little child, he shall not enter
therein." Christ's teaching was not that there is
something in us to fit us for the kingdom; and
that a certain number of years may make us capable
of receiving grace. His teaching all went the other
way—namely, that we are to be nothing, and that
the less we are and the weaker we are, the better;
for the less we have of self the more room there is
for His divine grace. Do you think to come to
Jesus up the ladder of knowledge? Come down;
you will meet Him at the foot. Do you think to
reach Jesus up the steep hill of experience! Come
down, dear climber; He stands in the plain. " Oh!
but when I am old, I shall then be prepared for
Christ." Stay where thou art, young man; Jesus

meets thee at the door of life; you were never more fit to meet Him than just now. He asks nothing of you but that you will be nothing, and that He may be all in all to you. That is His teaching: and to send back the child because it has not this or that is to fly in the teeth of the blessed doctrine of the grace of God.

Once more, it was quite contrary to Jesus Christ's practice. He made them see this; for "He took them up in His arms, put His hands upon them and blessed them." All His life long there is nothing in Him like rejection and refusing. He said truly, "Him that cometh to Me I will in no wise cast out." If He did cast out any because they were too young, the text would be falsified at once: but that can never be. He is the receiver of all who come to Him. It is written, "This Man receiveth sinners, and eateth with them." All His life He might be drawn as a shepherd with a lamb in His bosom: never as a cruel shepherd setting his dogs upon the lambs and driving them and their mothers away.

THE DISCIPLES AND THE MOTHERS.

HE immediate disciples of our Lord were a highly honourable band of men; despite their mistakes and shortcomings, they must have been greatly sweetened by living near to one so perfect and so full of love. I gather, therefore, that if these men, who were the cream of the cream, rebuked the mothers who brought their young children to Christ, it must be a pretty common offence in the church of God. I fear that the chilling frost of this mistake is felt almost everywhere. I am not going to make any ungenerous statement; but I think if a little personal investigation were made many of us might find ourselves guilty upon this point, and might be led to cry with Pharaoh's butler, "I do remember my faults this day." Have we laid ourselves out for the conversion of children, as much as we have done for the conversion of grown-up-folks? What! Do you think me sarcastic? Do you lay yourselves out for anybody's conversion? What must I say to you? It is dreadful that the Cainite spirit should enter a believer's heart and make him say,

"Am I my brother's keeper?" It is a shocking thing that we should ourselves eat the fat, and drink the sweet, and leave the famishing multitudes to perish. But tell me now, if you did care for the salvation of souls, would you not think it rather too commonplace a matter to begin with boys and girls? Yes; and your feeling is shared by many. The fault is common.

I believe, however, that this feeling, in the case of the apostles, was caused by zeal for Jesus. These good men thought that the bringing of children to the Saviour would cause an interruption: He was engaged in much better work: He had been confounding the Pharisees, instructing the masses, and healing the sick. Could it be right to pester Him with children? The little ones would not understand His teaching, and they did not need His miracles: why should they be brought in to disturb His great doings? Therefore the disciples as good as said, "Take your children back, good women. Teach them the law yourselves, and instruct them in the Psalms and the Prophets, and pray with them. Every child cannot have Christ's hands laid on it. If we suffer one set of children to come, we shall have all the neighbourhood swarming about us, and the Saviour's work will be grievously interrupted. Do you not see this? Why do you act so thoughtlessly?" The disciples had such reverence for their Master that they would send the prattlers away, lest the great Rabbi should seem to become a mere teacher of babes. This may have been a zeal for God, but it was not according to knowledge.   Thus in these days certain brethren would hardly like to receive many children into the church, lest it should become a society of boys and girls.   Surely, if these come into the church in any great numbers, the church may be spoken of in terms of reproach!   The outside world will call it a mere Sunday-school.   I remember that when a fallen woman had been converted in one of our county-towns, there was an objection among certain professors to her being received into the church, and certain lewd fellows of the baser sort even went the length of advertising upon the walls the fact that the Baptist minister had baptized a harlot.   I told my friend to regard it as an honour. Even so, if any reproach us with receiving young children into the church, we will wear the reproach as a badge of honour.   Holy children cannot possibly do us any harm.   God will send us sufficient of age and experience to steer the church prudently.   We will receive none who fail to yield evidence of the new birth, however old they may be ;   but we will shut out no believers, however young they may be.   God forbid that we should condemn our cautious brethren, but at the same time we wish their caution would show itself where it is more required.   Jesus will not be dishonoured by the children : we have far more cause to fear the adults.

The apostles' rebuke of the children arose in measure from ignorance of the children's need.   If any mother in that throng had said, " I must bring my child to the Master, for he is sore afflicted with a devil," neither Peter, nor James, nor John, would have demurred for a moment, but would have assisted in bringing the possessed child to the Saviour. Or suppose another mother had said, "My child has a pining sickness upon it, it is wasted to skin and bone ; permit me to bring my darling, that Jesus may lay His hands upon her,"—the disciples would all have said : " Make way for this woman and her sorrowful burden." But these little ones with bright eyes, and prattling tongues, and leaping limbs, why should they come to Jesus ? They forgot that in those children, with all their joy, their health, and their apparent innocence, there was a great and grievous need for the blessing of a Saviour's grace. If you indulge in the novel idea that *your* children do not need conversion, that children born of Christian parents are somewhat superior to others, and have good within them which only needs development, one great motive for your devout earnestness will be gone. Believe me, your children need the Spirit of God to give them new hearts and right spirits, or else they will go astray as other children do. Remember that however young they are, there is a stone within the youngest breast ; and that stone must be taken away, or be the ruin of the child. There is a tendency to evil even where as yet it is not developed into act, and that tendency needs to be overcome by the divine power of the Holy Spirit causing the child to be born again. Oh, that the church of God would cast off the old Jewish idea which still has such force around us—namely, that

natural birth brings with it covenant privileges!
Now, even under the Old Dispensation there were
hints that the true seed was not born after the
flesh, but after the spirit, as in the case of Ishmael
and Isaac, and Esau and Jacob. Will not even the
church of God know that "That which is born of the
flesh is flesh; and that which is born of the Spirit
is spirit"? "Who can bring a clean thing out of
an unclean?" The natural birth communicates
nature's filthiness, but it cannot convey grace.
Under the new covenant we are expressly told
that the sons of God are "born not of blood,
nor of the will of the flesh, nor of the will of
man, but of God." Under the old covenant,
which was typical, the birth according to the flesh
yielded privilege; but to come at all under the
covenant of grace ye must be born again. The
first birth brings you nothing but an inheritance
with the first Adam; you must be born again to
come under the headship of the second Adam.

But it is written, saith one, "that the promise is
unto you, and to your children." There never was
a grosser piece of knavery committed under heaven
than the quotation of that text as it is usually
quoted. I have heard it quoted many times to
prove a doctrine which is very far removed from that
which it clearly teaches. If you take one half of
any sentence which a man utters, and leave out the
rest, you may make him say the opposite of what
he means. What do you think that text really is?
See Acts ii. 39: " The promise is unto you, and to
your children, and to all that are afar off, even as

many as the Lord our God shall call." This grandly wide statement is the argument on which is founded the exhortation, "Repent, and be baptized every one of you." It is not a declaration of privilege special to anyone, but a presentation of grace as much to all that are afar off as to them and to their children. There is not a word in the New Testament to show that the benefits of divine grace are in any degree transmitted by natural descent : they come "to as many as the Lord our God shall call," whether their parents are saints or sinners. How can people have the impudence to tear off half a text to make it teach what is not true ? You must sorrowfully look upon your children as born in sin, and shapen in iniquity, "heirs of wrath, even as others " ; and though you may yourself belong to a line of saints, and trace your pedigree from minister to minister, all eminent in the church of God, yet your children occupy precisely the same position by their birth as other people's children do ; so that they must be redeemed from under the curse of the law by the precious blood of Jesus, and they must receive a new nature by the work of the Holy Ghost. They are favoured by being placed under godly training, and under the hearing of the gospel ; but their need and their sinfulness are the same as in the rest of the race. If you think of this, you will see the reason why they should be brought to Jesus Christ—a reason why they should be brought as speedily as possible in the arms of your prayer and faith to Him who is able to renew them.

I have sometimes met with a deeper spiritual experience in children of ten and twelve than I have in certain persons of fifty and sixty. It is an old proverb that some children are born with beards. Some boys are little men, and some girls are little old women. You cannot measure the lives of any of us by our ages. I knew a boy who, when he was fifteen, often heard old Christian people say, " The boy is sixty years old : he speaks with such insight into divine truth." I believe that this youth at fifteen did know far more of the things of God, and of soul travail, than any around him, whatever their age might be. I cannot tell you why it is, but so I do know it is, that some are old when they are young, and some are very green when they are old ; some are wise when you would expect them to be otherwise, and others are very foolish when you might have expected that they had quitted their folly. Talk not of a child's incapacity for repentance ! I have known a child weep herself to sleep by the month together under a crushing sense of sin. If you would know a deep, and bitter, and awful fear of the wrath of God, let me tell you what I felt as a boy. If you would know joy in the Lord, many a child has been as full of it as his little heart could hold. If you want to know what faith in Jesus is, you must not look to those who have been bemuddled by the heretical jargon of the times, but to the dear children who have taken Jesus at His word, and believed in Him, and loved Him, and therefore know and are sure that they are saved. Capacity for believing lies more in the child than in the man. We grow less rather than more capable of faith : every year brings the unregenerate mind further away from God, and makes it less capable of receiving the things of God. No ground is more prepared for the good seed than that which as yet has not been trodden down as the highway, nor has been as yet over-grown with thorns. Not yet has the child learned the deceits of pride, the falsehood of ambition, the delusions of worldliness, the tricks of trade, the sophistries of philosophy ; and so far it has an advantage over the adult. In any case the new birth is the work of the Holy Ghost, and He can as easily work upon youth as upon age.

Some, too, have hindered the children because they have been forgetful of the child's value. The soul's price does not depend upon its years. "Oh, it is only a child!" "Children are a nuisance." "Children are always getting in the way." This talk is common. God forgive those who despise the little ones! Will you be very angry if I say that a boy is more worth saving than a man? It is infinite mercy on God's part to save those who are seventy ; for what good can they now do with the fag-end of their lives? When we get to be fifty or sixty, we are almost worn out ; and if we have spent all our early days with the devil, what remains for God? But these dear boys and girls —there is something to be made out of them. If now they yield themselves to Christ they may have a long, happy, and holy day before them in which they may serve God with all their hearts. Who

knows what glory God may have of them?
Heathen lands may call them blessed. Whole
nations may be enlightened by them. If a
famous schoolmaster was accustomed to take
his hat off to his boys because he did not know
whether one of them might not be Prime Minister,
we may justly look upon converted children, for
we do not know how soon they may be among the
angels, or how greatly their light may shine among
men. Let us estimate children at their true
valuation, and we shall not keep them back, but
we shall be eager to lead them to Jesus at once.

In proportion to our own spirituality of mind,
and in proportion to our own child-likeness of heart,
we shall be at home with children ; and we shall
enter into their early fears and hopes, their budding
faith and opening love. Dwelling among young
converts, we shall seem to be in a garden of flowers,
in a vineyard where the tender grapes give a good
smell.

THE CHILDREN'S SHEPHERD.

SIMON Peter was not a Welshman, but he had a great deal of what we know as Welsh fire in him. He was just the sort of man to interest the young. Children delight to gather round a fire, whether it be on the hearth or in the heart. Certain persons appear to be made of ice, and from these children speedily shrink away: congregations or classes grow smaller every Sunday when cold-blooded creatures preside over them. But when a man or a woman has a kindly heart, the children seem to gather readily, just as flies in autumn days swarm on a warm, sunny wall. Therefore Jesus says to warm-hearted Simon, "Feed My lambs." He is the man for the office.

Simon Peter was, moreover, an experienced man. He had known his own weakness ; he had felt the pangs of conscience ; he had sinned much and had been much forgiven, and now he was brought in tender humility to confess the love and loveliness of Jesus. We want experienced men and women to talk to converted children, and to tell them what the Lord has done for them, and what have been their dangers, their sins, their sorrows, and their comforts. The young are glad to hear the story of those who have been further on the road than they have. I may say of experienced saints—their lips keep knowledge. Experience lovingly narrated is suitable food for young believers, instruction such as the Lord is likely to bless to their nourishing in grace.

Simon Peter was now a greatly indebted man. He owed much to Jesus Christ, according to that rule of the Kingdom—he loveth much to whom much hath been forgiven. Oh, you that have never entered upon this service for Christ, and yet might do it well, come forward at once and say, " I have left this work to younger hands, but I will do so no longer. I have experience, and I trust I yet retain a warm heart within my bosom ; I will go and join these workers, who are steadily feeding the lambs in the name of the Lord." So far as to the man who is called to feed the lambs.

When the Lord calls a man to a work, He gives him the preparation necessary for it. How was Peter prepared for feeding Christ's lambs ? First, *by being fed himself*. The Lord gave him a breakfast before giving him a commission. You cannot feed lambs, or sheep either, unless you are fed yourself. It is quite right for you to be teaching a great part of the Lord's-day ; but I think a teacher is very unwise who does not come to hear the gospel preached and get a meal for his own soul. First be fed, and then feed.

But especially Peter was prepared for feeding

the lambs by *being with his Master*. He would never forget that morning, and all the incidents of it. It was Christ's voice that he heard ; it was Christ's look that pierced him to the heart ; he breathed the air which surrounded the risen Lord, and this fellowship with Jesus perfumed Peter's heart and tuned Peter's speech, that he might afterwards go forth and feed the lambs. I commend to you the study of instructive books, but above all I commend the study of Christ. Let Him be your library. Get near to Jesus. An hour's communion with Jesus is the best preparation for teaching either the young or the old.

Peter was also prepared in a more painful way than that—namely, by self-examination. The question came to him thrice over, " Simon, son of Jonas, lovest thou Me ? Lovest thou Me ? Lovest thou Me ? " Often the vessel wants scouring with self-examination before the Lord can fitly use it to convey the living water to thirsting ones. It never hurts a true-hearted man to search his own spirit, and to be searched and tried by his Lord. It is the hypocrite who is afraid of the truth which tests his profession : trying discourses, and trying meditations, he dreads ; but the genuine man wants to know for certain that he really does love Christ, and therefore he looks within him and questions and cross-questions himself.

Mainly that examination should be exercised concerning our love ; for the best preparation for teaching Christ's lambs is love,—love to Jesus and to them. We cannot be priests on their behalf unless like Aaron we wear their names upon our breasts. We must love or we cannot bless. Teaching is poor work when love is gone ; it is like a smith working without fire, or a builder without mortar. A shepherd who does not love his sheep is a hireling and not a shepherd : he will flee in the time of danger, and leave his flock to the wolf. Where there is no love there will be no life ; living lambs are not to be fed by dead men. We preach and teach love : our subject is the love of God in Christ Jesus. How can we teach this if we have no love ourselves ? Our object is to create love in the hearts of those we teach, and to foster it where it already exists ; but how can we convey the fire if it is not kindled in our own hearts ? How can he promote the flame whose hands are damp, and dripping with worldliness and indifference, so that he acts on the child's heart rather as a bucket of water than as a flame of fire ? These lambs of the flock live in the love of Christ : shall they not live in ours ? He calls them His lambs, and so they are ; shall we not love them for His sake ? They were chosen in love ; they were redeemed in love ; they have been called in love ; they have been washed in love ; they have been fed by love, and they will be kept by love till they come to the green pastures on the hilltops of heaven. You and I will be out of gear with the vast machinery of divine love unless our souls are full of affectionate zeal for the good of the beloved ones. Love is the grandest preparation for the ministry, whether exercised in the congregation or in the class.

Love, and then feed. If thou lovest, feed. If thou dost not love, then wait till the Lord hath quickened thee, and lay not thy unhallowed hand to this sacred service.

With the weak of the flock, with the new converts in the flock, with the young children in the flock, our principal business is to feed. Every sermon, every lesson, should be a feeding sermon and a feeding lesson. It is of little use to stand and thump the Bible and call out, "Believe, believe, believe!" when nobody knows what is to be believed. I see no use in fiddles and tambourines; neither lambs nor sheep can be fed upon brass bands. There must be doctrine, solid, sound, gospel doctrine to constitute real feeding. When you have a joint on the table, then ring the dinner-bell; but the bell feeds nobody if no provender is served up. Getting children to meet in the morning and the afternoon is a waste of their steps and yours if you do not set before them soul-saving, soul-sustaining truth. Feed the lambs; you need not pipe to them, nor put garlands round their necks; but do feed them.

This feeding is humble, lowly, unostentatious work. Do you know the name of a shepherd? I have known the names of one or two who follow that calling, but I never heard anybody speak of them as great men; their names are not in the papers, nor do we hear of them as a trade with a grievance, claiming to be noticed by the legislature. Shepherds are generally quiet, unobtrusive people. When you look at the shepherd, you would not see any difference between him and the ploughman, or the carter. He plods on uncomplainingly through the winter, and in the early spring he has no rest night or day because the lambs are needing him : this he does year after year, and yet he will never be made a Knight of the Garter, nor even be exalted to the peerage, albeit he may have done far more useful work than those who are floated into rank upon their own beer-barrels. So in the case of many a faithful teacher of young children ; you hear but little about him, yet he is doing grand work for which future ages will call him blessed. His Master knows all about him, and we shall hear of him in that day ; perhaps not till then.

Feeding the lambs is _careful work_, too ; for lambs cannot be fed on anything you please, especially Christ's lambs. You can soon half poison young believers with bad teaching. Christ's lambs are all too apt to eat herbs which are deleterious ; it needs that we be cautious where we lead them. If men are to take heed what they hear, how much more should we take heed what we teach. It is careful work the feeding of each lamb separately, and the teaching of each child by itself the truth which it is best able to receive.

Moreover, this is continuous work. " Feed My lambs," is not for a season, but for all time. Lambs could not live if the shepherd only fed them once a week. I reckon they would die between Sunday and Sunday ; therefore good teachers of the young look after them all the days of the week as they have opportunity, and they are careful about their souls with prayer and holy example when they are not teaching them by word of mouth. The shepherdry of lambs is daily, hourly work. When is a shepherd's work over? How many hours a day does he labour? He will tell you that in lambing-time he is never done. He sleeps between whiles just when he can, taking much less than forty winks, and then rousing himself for action. It is so with those who feed Christ's lambs; they rest not till God saves and sanctifies their dear ones.

It is laborious work, too; at least, he who does not labour at it will have a terrible account to render. Do you think a minister's life is an easy one? I tell you that he who makes it so will find it hard enough when he comes to die. Nothing so exhausts a man who is called to it as the care of souls; so it is in measure with all who teach—they cannot do good without spending themselves. You must study the lesson; you must bring forth something fresh to your class: you must instruct and impress. I have no doubt you are often driven very hard for matter, and wonder how you will get through the next Lord's-day. I know you are sore pressed at times if you are worth your salt. You dare not rush to your class unprepared and offer to the Lord that which costs you nothing. There must be labour if the food is to be wisely placed before the lambs, so that they can receive it.

And all this has to be done in a singularly choice spirit; the true shepherd spirit is an amalgam of many precious graces. He is hot with zeal, but he is not fiery with passion; he is gentle, and yet he rules his class; he is loving, but he does not wink at sin ; he has power over the lambs, but he is not domineering or sharp ; he has cheerfulness, but not levity ; freedom, but not license ; solemnity, but not gloom. He who cares for lambs should be a lamb himself ; and blessed be God, there is a Lamb before the throne who cares for all of us, and does so the more effectually because He is in all things made like unto us. The shepherd spirit is a rare and priceless gift. A successful pastor or a successful teacher in a school will be found to have special characteristics, which distinguish him from his fellows. A bird when it is sitting on its eggs, or when the little ones are newly-hatched, has about it a mother-spirit, so that it devotes all its life to the feeding of its little ones : other birds may be taking their pleasure on the wing, but this bird sits still the life-long day and night, or else its only flights are to provide for gaping mouths which seem to be never filled. A passion has taken possession of the bird ; and something like it comes over the true soul-winner : he would gladly die to win souls ; he pines, he pleads, he plods to bless those on whom his heart is set. If these could but be saved he would pawn half his heaven for it ; ay, and sometimes in moments of enthusiasm he is ready to barter heaven altogether to win souls, and, like Paul, he could wish himself accursed, so that they were but saved. This blessed extravagance many cannot understand, because they never felt it ; may the Holy Ghost work it in us, so shall we act as true shepherds towards the lambs. This, then, is the work : " Feed My lambs."

OF SUCH IS THE KINGDOM OF HEAVEN.

OUR Lord tells the disciples that the gospel sets up a kingdom. Was there ever a kingdom which had no children in it? How, then, could it grow? Jesus tells us that children are admitted into the kingdom; nay, not only that some few are here and there admitted into it, but, "of such is the kingdom of God." I am not inclined to get away from the plain sense of that expression, nor to suggest that He merely means that the kingdom consists of those who are like children. It is clear that He intended such children as those who were before him—babes and young children: "of such is the kingdom of God." There are children in all kingdoms, and there are children in Christ's kingdom; and I am not certain that John Newton was not right when he said that the majority of persons who are now in the kingdom of God are children. When I think of all the multitudes of babes that have died, who are now swarming in the streets of heaven, it does seem to me to be a blessed thought that albeit generation after generation of adults

have passed away in unbelief and rebellion, yet
enormous multitudes of children have gone stream-
ing up to heaven, saved by the grace of God, through
the death of Christ, to sing the high praises of the
Lord for ever before the eternal throne. " Of such
is the kingdom of heaven." They give tone and
character to the kingdom ; it is rather a kingdom
of children than of men.

Our Lord tells us that the way of entering the
kingdom is by receiving. " Whosoever shall not
receive the kingdom of God as a little child shall
in no wise enter therein." We do not enter into the
kingdom of God by working out some deep pro-
blem and arriving at its solution ; not by fetching
something out of ourselves, but by receiving a
secret something into us. We come into the king
dom by the kingdom's coming into us : it receives
us by our receiving it. Now, if this entrance into
the kingdom depended upon something to be
fetched out of the human mind by study and deep
thought, then very few children could ever enter
it ; but it depends upon something to be received,
and therefore children may enter. Those children
who are of years sufficient to sin, and to be saved
by faith, have to listen to the gospel and to receive
it by faith : and they can do this, God the Holy
Spirit helping them. There is no doubt about it,
because great numbers have done it. I will not
say at what age children are first capable of receiving
the knowledge of Christ, but it is much earlier than
some fancy ; and we have seen and known children
who have given abundant evidence that they have

received Christ and have believed in Him at a very early age. Some of them have died triumphantly, and others of them have lived graciously, and some are here now, grown up to be men and women, who are honourable members of the church.

We know that infants enter the kingdom, for we are convinced that all of our race who die in infancy are included in the election of grace, and partake in the redemption wrought out by our Lord Jesus. Whatever some may think, the whole spirit and tone of the Word of God, as well as the nature of God Himself, lead us to believe that all who leave this world as babes are saved. Now, how do they receive the kingdom, for in the same way must we receive it? Certainly children do not receive it by birth or blood, for we are expressly told in John's gospel that the children of God are born not of blood nor of the will of the flesh. All privilege of descent is now abolished, and no babe enters into heaven because it was born of a pious father or mother, neither shall any be shut out because his progenitors were atheists or idolaters. My solemn persuasion is that the child of a Mahomedan, or a Papist, or a Buddhist, or a cannibal, dying in infancy, is as surely saved as the child of the Christian. Salvation by blood or birth there can be none, for the gospel dispensation does not admit of it : if saved, as we assuredly believe they are, infants must be saved simply according to the will and good pleasure of God, because He hath made them to be His own.

Children dying in infancy in China and Japan

are as truly saved as those dying in England or
Scotland. Babes of swarthy mothers, infants born
in the kraal of the Hottentot or the wigwam of
the Red Indian are alike saved, and therefore not
saved by any outward rite, or by the mystic power
of a priesthood. They are raised to the kingdom
of heaven by the free and sovereign grace of God.
How are they saved, then ? By works ? No, for
they have never wrought any. By their natural
innocence ? No ; for if that innocence could have
admitted them to heaven, it must also have sufficed
to save them from pain and death. If sin be not
upon them in some form, how is it that they suffer ?
The imputed sin which makes them die prevents
our believing that they claim heaven by right of
innocence. They die because of Adam's fall. Sad
consequences of their being born of fallen parents.
Mark their appealing looks as the dear little ones
look up in their sufferings, as if they would fain
ask why they must endure so much pain. We look
at them with all the deeper grief because we cannot
help them, and are made to reflect upon the mysterious union of the race in its fall and sorrow. The
anguish of the dying little one is a proof of Adam's
fall, and of its participation in the result thereof.
The dear babes live again, however, because Jesus
died and rose again, and they are in Him. They
perish, as far as this life is concerned, for a sin which
they did not commit : but they also live eternally
through a righteousness in which they had no hand,
even the righteousness of Jesus Christ, who hath
redeemed them. We know little of the matter,

but we suppose them to undergo regeneration ere they enter heaven : for that which is born of the flesh is flesh, and to enter the spiritual world they must be born of the Spirit. But whatever is wrought in them, it is clear that they do not enter the kingdom by the force of intellect, or will, or merit, but as a matter of free grace, having no reference to anything that they have done or have felt. In that same manner you must pass into the kingdom entirely through free grace, and not at all by any power or merit of your own. You will enter heaven as fully by grace as if you had never lived a godly life, nor had practised a single virtue.

Now we have to think of another sort of children, those who outlive the time of infancy and become children capable of actual sin, and of knowing Christ, and being converted. Many of these by faith enter the kingdom. Now, as these children receive the kingdom of heaven, so must we receive it. How do the children receive it ? I answer, a child receives the gospel with humility, with simple faith, and with unworldliness. Children are not held up to us as an example in all things, for they have faults which we ought to avoid, but they are here praised in this point,—the way in which they receive the kingdom. How does a child receive it ? First, with humility. He is humble enough to be without prejudice. Take a little child and tell him about Christ Jesus the Saviour, and if God blesses the telling of the story of the cross, and he believes it, he receives it without having any wrong views and notions to battle with. Many a man goes to

hear the gospel with the idea that Christ is merely
human ; he cannot get rid of that prejudice from
his mind, and therefore he does not receive Christ
Jesus the Lord.   Another comes to hear the word
with the recollection of all that he has heard and
read of infidelity, heresy, and profanity : how can
he profit till this is removed ?   Another comes with
his mind stuffed with proud self-righteousness,
with a belief in priestcraft, or with a reliance upon
some form or ceremony.   If we could get this
lumber out of the soul, there would be some hope ;
but all this is a hindrance.   Now, the dear child,
as he listens to the story of the love of God in
Christ Jesus, has none of these prejudices to spoil
his hearing.   Very likely he does not even know
that such evils have been invented by man, and he
is blessed in his ignorance.   He will find out the
evil soon enough ; but for the present he humbly
drinks in the word, and prays,—

> " Gentle Jesus, meek and mild,
> Look on me, a little child !
> Pity my simplicity ;
> Suffer me to come to Thee."

Now, this deliverance from preconceived notions
is what we greatly need.   Just as your little boy or
your little girl must believe, even so must you.
There is only one way for the shepherd and the
sage, the philosopher and the peasant.   The little
child receives Christ humbly, for he never dreams
of merit or purchase.   I do not recollect ever
having met with a child who had to battle with
self-righteousness in coming to Christ.

AS A LITTLE CHILD.[*]

WHEN our Lord blessed the little children He was making His last journey to Jerusalem. It was thus a farewell blessing which He gave to the little ones, and it reminds us of the fact that among His parting words to His disciples, before He was taken up, we find the tender charge, " Feed My lambs." The ruling passion was strong upon the great Shepherd of Israel, "who gathereth the lambs with His arm, and carrieth them in His bosom " ; and it was fitting that while He was making His farewell journey He should bestow His gracious benediction upon the children.

Our Lord Jesus Christ is not among us in person ; but we know where He is, and we know that He is clothed with all power in heaven and in earth wherewith to bless His people ; let us then draw near to Him. Let us seek His touch in the form of fellowship, and ask the aid of His intercession ; let us include others in our prayers, and among these let us give our children, and, indeed, all children, a leading place. We know more of Jesus than the women of Palestine did ; let us, therefore, be even more eager than they were to bring our children to Him that He may bless them, and that they may be accepted in Him, even as we ourselves are. Jesus waits to bless. He is not changed in character, or impoverished in grace ; as He still receiveth sinners, so doth He still bless children ; and let none of us be content, whether we be parents or teachers, until He has received our children, and has so blessed them that we are sure that they have entered the kingdom of God.

Our Saviour, when He saw that His disciples were not only backward to admit the children to Him, but even rebuked those who brought them, was much displeased, and called them to Him that He might teach them better. He then informed them that, instead of the children being regarded as intruders, they were most welcome to Himself ; and, instead of being interlopers, they had full right of access, for of children and of childlike persons His kingdom was composed. Moreover, He declared that none could enter that kingdom except in the same manner as children enter. He spoke with divine certainty, using His own expressive " verily," and He spoke with the weight of His own personal authority, " I say unto you." These prefatory expressions are intended to secure our reverent attention to the fact that so far from the admission of children into the kingdom being unusual or strange, none can find entrance there except they receive the gospel as a little child receives it.

It is pretty clear that the disciples thought the children were too insignificent for the Lord's time to be taken up by them. If it had been a prince who wished to come to Jesus, no doubt Peter and the rest of them would have diligently secured him an introduction ; but, you see, these were only poor women, with babes, and boys, and girls. If it had been an ordinary person, like themselves, they would not have repelled him with rebukes. But mere children ! Sucklings and little children ! It was too bad for these to be intruded upon the great Teacher. A word is used about the youthful applicants which may signify children of any age, from sucklings up to twelve years : surely Jesus had worry enough without the intrusion of these juveniles. He had higher subjects for thought, and graver objects of care. The children were so very little, they were quite beneath His notice : so the disciples thought in their hearts. But if it comes to a matter of insignificance, who can hope to win the divine attention ? If we think that children must be little in His sight, what are we ? He taketh up the isles as a very little thing ; the inhabitants of the earth are as grasshoppers ; yea, we are all as things of nought. If we were humble we should exclaim, " Lord, what is man, that Thou art mindful of him ? and the son of man, that Thou visitest him ? " If we dream that the Lord will not notice the little and insignificant, what think we of

such a text as this—"Are not two sparrows sold for
a farthing? and one of them shall not fall on the
ground without your Father"; doth God care for
sparrows, and shall He not care for little children?
The idea of insignificance must be set aside at once.
"Though the Lord be high, yet hath He respect
unto the lowly." But are little children so insignificant? Do they not people heaven? Is it not
your conviction? it is mine—that they make up a
very considerable part of the population of the
skies. Multitudes of infant feet are treading the
streets of the New Jerusalem. Snatched from the
breast ere they had committed actual sin, delivered
from the toilsome pilgrimage of life, they always
behold the face of our Father which is in heaven.
"Of such is the kingdom of God." Call you these
insignificant? Children, who are the most numer-
ous company in the army of the elect, dare you
despise them? I might turn the tables, and call
the adults insignificant, among whom there can be
found no more than a small remnant who serve the
Lord. Besides, many children are spared to grow
up to man's estate, and therefore we must not think
a child insignificant. He is the father of the man.
In him are great possibilities and capacities. His
manhood is as yet undeveloped but it is there, and
he that trifles with it mars the man. He who
tempts the mind of a boy may destroy the soul of a
man. A little error injected into the ear of a youth
may become deadly in the man when the slow
poison shall at last have touched a vital part. Weeds
sown in the furrows of childhood will grow with the

young man's growth, ripen in his prime, and only decay into a sad corruption when he himself declines. On the other hand, a truth dropped into a child's heart will there fructify, and his manhood shall see the fruit of it. Yon child listening in the class to his teacher's gentle voice may develop into a Luther, and shake the world with his vehement proclamation of the truth. Who among us can tell ? At any rate, with the truth in his heart the boy shall grow up to honour and fear the Lord, and thus shall he help to keep alive a godly seed in these evils days. Therefore let no man despise the young, or think them insignificant. I claim a front place for them. I ask that, if others are kept back, at any rate their feebleness may make room for the little ones. They are the world's future. The past has been and we cannot alter it ; even the present is gone while we gaze on it ; but our hope lies in the future : therefore, by your leave, room for the children, room for the boys and girls !

I suppose that these grown-up apostles thought that the children's minds were too trifling. They are at their play and their childish mirth : they will regard it only as a pastime to be folded in Jesus' arms ; it will be mirth to them, and they will have no idea of the solemnity of their position. Well ! well ! Trifling, is it ? Children are said to be guilty of trifling ! Are not ye also triflers ? If it comes to an examination upon the matter of trifling, who are the greatest triflers, children or full-grown men and women ? What is greater trifling than for a man to live for the enjoyment of sensual pleasures, or for a woman to live to dress herself and waste her time in company? Nay, more, what is the accumulation of wealth for the sake of it but miserable trifling? Child's play without the amusement! Most men are triflers on a larger scale than children, and that is the main difference. Children when they trifle play with little things—their toys so breakable, are they not made on purpose to be trifled with and broken? The child with his trifles is but doing as he should. Alas, I know men and women who trifle with their souls, and with heaven and hell, and eternity; they trifle with God's Word, trifle with God's Son, trifle with God Himself! Charge not children with being frivolous, for their little games often have as much of earnestness about them, and are as useful, as the pursuits of men. Half the councils of our senators and the debates of our parliaments are worse than child's play. The game of war is a far greater folly than the most frolicsome of boyish tricks. Big children are worse triflers than the little ones can ever be. Despise not children for trifling when the whole world is given to folly.

" Ay," say they, " but if we should let the children come to Christ, and if He should bless them, they will soon forget it. No matter how loving His look and How spiritual His words, they will go back to their play, and their weak memories will preserve no trace of it at all." This objection we meet in the same manner as the others. Do not men forget? What a forgetful generation do most preachers address! Verily this is a generation like to that of which Isaiah said, " Precept must be upon precept, precept upon precept ; line upon line, line upon line ; here a little, and there a little." Alas ! many must have the gospel preached to them again, and again, and again, till the preacher is well nigh weary with his hopeless task ; for they are like to men who see their natural faces in a glass, and go their way to forget what manner of men they are. They live in sin still. The Word has no abiding place in their hearts. Forgetfulness ! Charge not children with it lest the accusation be proven against yourselves.

But do the little ones forget ? I suppose the events which we best remember in advanced age are the things which happened to us in our earliest days. At any rate, I have shaken hands with grey-headed men who have forgotten nearly all the events which have intervened between their old age and the time of their childhood, but little matters which transpired at home, hymns learned at their mother's knee, and words spoken by their father or sister, have lingered with them. The voices of childhood echo throughout life. The first learned is generally the last forgotten. The young children who heard our Lord's blessing would not forget it. They would have His coun-tenance photographed upon their hearts, and never forget His kind and tender smile. Peter, and James, and John, and the rest of you, are all mis-taken, and therefore you must suffer the children to come to Jesus.

Perhaps, too, they thought that children had not

sufficient capacity. Jesus Christ said such wonderful
things that the children could not be supposed to
have the capacity to receive them. Yet, indeed,
this is a great error ; for children readily enter into
our Lord's teaching. They never learn to read so
quickly from any book as from the New Testament.
The words of Jesus are so childlike and so fitted
for children that they drink them in better than the
words of any other man, however simple he may
try to be. Children readily understand the child
Jesus. What is this matter of capacity ? What
capacity is wanted ? Capacity to believe ? I tell
you, children have more of that than grown-up
persons. I am not now speaking of the spiritual
part of faith, but as far as the mental faculty is
concerned, there is any quantity of the capacity for
faith in the heart of a child. His believing faculty
has not yet been overloaded by superstition, or per-
verted by falsehood, or maimed by wicked unbelief.
Only let the Holy Spirit consecrate the faculty, and
there is enough of it for the production of abundant
faith in God.

In what respect are children deficient of capacity ?
Do they lack capacity for repentance ? Assuredly
not : have I not seen a girl weep herself ill because
she has done wrong? A tender conscience in many
a little boy has made him unutterably miserable
when he has been conscious of a fault. Do not
some of us recollect the keen arrows of conviction
which rankled in our hearts when we were yet
children ? I distinctly recollect the time when I
could not rest because of sin, and sought the Lord,

while yet a child, with bitter anguish. Children are capable enough of repentance, God the Holy Spirit working it in them : this is no conjecture, for we ourselves are living witnesses.

What, then, do children want in the matter of capacity? "Why, they have not sufficient understanding," says one.   Understanding—of what? If the religion of Jesus were that of Modern Thought, if it were such sublime nonsense that none but the so-called cultured class could make head or tail of it, then children might be incapable of its comprehension ; but if it be indeed the gospel of the poor man's Bible, then there are shallows in it where the tiniest lamb in Jesus' fold may wade without fear of being carried off its feet. It is true that in the Scriptures there are great mysteries, where your leviathans may dive and find no bottom ; but the knowledge of these deep things is not essential to salvation, or else few of us would be saved. The things that are essential to salvation are so exceedingly simple that no child need sit down in despair of understanding the things which make for his peace. Christ crucified is not a riddle for sages, but a plain truth for plain people : true, it is meat for men, but it is also milk for babes.

Did you say that children could not love ? That, after all, is one of the grandest parts of the education of a Christian ; did you dream that children could not attain to it? No, you did not say that, nor dared you think it, for the capacity for love is great in a child. Would God it were always as great in ourselves !

4

To put the thoughts of the apostles into one or two words : they thought that the children must not come to Christ because they were not like themselves—they were not men and women. A child not big enough, tall enough, grown enough, great enough to be blessed by Jesus ! So they half thought. The child must not come to the Master because he is not like the man. How the blessed Saviour turns the tables and says, "Say not, the child may not come till he is like a man, but know that *you* cannot come till you are like him. It is no difficulty in the child's way that he is not like you ; the difficulty is with you, that you are not like the child." Instead of the child needing to wait until he grows up and becomes a man, it is the man who must grow down and become like a child. "Whoever shall not receive the kingdom of God as a little child, shall in no wise enter therein." Our Lord's words are a complete and all-sufficient answer to the thoughts of His disciples, and we may each one as we read them learn wisdom. Let us not say, "Would to God my child were grown up like myself that he might come to Christ ! " but rather may we almost wish that we were little children again, could forget much that now we know, could be washed clean from habit and prejudice, and could begin again with a child's freshness, simplicity, and eagerness. As we pray for spiritual childhood, Scripture sets its seal upon the prayer, for it is written, " Except a man be born again he cannot see the kingdom of God " ; and again, " Except ye be converted, and become as little children, ye shall not enter into the kingdom of heaven."

Now, I wonder whether any have such a thought as the disciples' lingering in brain or heart? I wonder whether you ever think in this fashion? I should not be surprised if you do. I hope it is not quite so common as it used to be, but I used to see in certain quarters among old folks a deep suspicion of youthful piety. The seniors shook their heads at the idea of receiving children into the church. Some even ventured to speak of converts as "only a lot of girls and boys": as if they were the worse for that. Many if they hear of a child-convert are very dubious, unless he dies very soon, and then they believe all about him. If the child lives they sharpen their axes to have a cut at him by way of examination. He must know all the doctrines, certainly, and he must be supernaturally grave. It is not every grown-up person who knows the higher doctrines of the Word, but if the young person should not know them he is set aside. Some people expect almost infinite wisdom in a child before they can believe him to be the subject of Divine grace. This is monstrous. Then, again, if a believing child should act like a child, some of the fathers of the last generation judged that he could not be converted, as if conversion to Christ added twenty years to our age. Of course, the young convert must not play any more, nor talk in his own childish fashion, or the seniors would be shocked ; for it was a sort of understood thing that as soon as ever a child was converted he was to turn into an old man.

I never could see anything in Scripture to support
this theory ; but then Scripture was not so much
cared for as the judgment of the deep-experienced
people, and the general opinion that it was well to
summer and winter all converts before admitting
them into the sacred enclosures of the church.
Now, if any of you still have an idea in your head
hostile to the conversion of children, try and get
rid of it, for it is as wrong as wrong can be. If
there were two enquirers before me now, a child
and a man, and I received from each the same
testimony, I should have no more right to distrust
the child than to suspect the man : in fact, if suspicion must come in anywhere, it ought rather to
be exercised towards the adult than in reference to
the child, who is far less likely to be guilty of
hypocrisy than the man, and far less likely to have
borrowed his words and phrases.   At any rate,
learn from the Master's words that you are not to
try and make the child like yourself, but you are to
be transformed till you yourself are like the child.

FEED MY LAMBS.

HE motive for feeding the lambs was to be his Master's self, and not his own self. Had Peter been the first pope of Rome, and had he been like his successors, which indeed he never was, surely it would have been fitting for the Lord to have said to him, "Feed *your* sheep. I commit them to you, O Peter, Vicar of Christ on earth." No, no, no. Peter is to feed them, but they are not his, they are still Christ's. The work that you have to do for Jesus, brethren and sisters, is in no sense for yourselves. Your classes are not your children, but Christ's. The exhortation which Paul gave was, "Feed the church of God," and Peter himself wrote in his epistle, "Feed the flock of God which is among you, taking the oversight thereof, not by constraint, but willingly; not for filthy lucre, but of a ready mind." Let these lambs turn out what they may, the glory is to be to the Master and not to the servant; and the whole time spent, and labour given, and energy put forth, is every particle

of it to redound to His praise whose these lambs
are.

Yet while this is a self-denying occupation, it is
sweetly honourable, too, and we may attend to it
feeling that it is one of the noblest forms of service.
Jesus says, "_My_ lambs : _My_ sheep." Think of
them, and wonder that Jesus should commit them
to us. Poor Peter! Surely when that breakfast
began he felt awkward. I put myself into his place,
and I know I should hardly have liked to look
across the table to Jesus, as I remembered that I
denied Him with oaths and curses. Our Lord
desired to set Peter quite at his ease by leading
him to speak upon his love, which had been so
seriously placed in question. Like a good doctor
he puts in the lancet where the anxiety was
festering : He enquires, "Lovest thou Me?" It
was not because Jesus did not know Peter's love ;
but in order that Peter might know of a surety,
and make a new confession, saying, "Yea, Lord ;
Thou knowest that I love Thee." The Lord is
about to hold a tender controversy with the erring
one for a few minutes, that there might never be a
controversy between Him and Peter any more.
When Peter said, "Yea, Lord ; Thou knowest that
I love Thee," you half thought that the Lord would
answer, "Ah, Peter, and I love you"; but He did
not say so, and yet He did say so. Perhaps Peter
did not see His meaning ; but we can see it, for
our minds are not confused as Peter's was on that
memorable morning. Jesus did in effect say, "I
love you so that I trust you with that which I

purchased with My heart's blood. The dearest
thing I have in all the world is My flock : see,
Simon, I have such confidence in you, I so wholly
rely on your integrity as being a sincere lover of
Me, that I make you a shepherd to My sheep.
These are all I have on earth, I gave everything
for them, even My life ; and now, Simon, son of
Jonas, take care of them for Me." Oh, it was
" kindly spoken." It was the great heart of Christ
saying, " Poor Peter, come right in and share My
dearest cares." Jesus so belicved Peter's declaration
that He did not tell him so in words, but in deeds.
Three times He said it, "Feed My lambs : feed My
sheep, feed My sheep," to show how much He loved
him. When the Lord Jesus loves a man very
much, He gives him much to do or much to suffer.

Many of us have been plucked like brands from
the burning, for we were "enemies to God by
wicked works " ; and now we are in the church
among His friends, and our Saviour trusts us with
His dearest ones. I wonder when the prodigal son
came back and the father received him, whether
when market-day came he sent his younger son to
market to sell the wheat and bring home the
money. Most of you would have said, "I am
glad the boy is come back ; at the same time, I
shall send his elder brother to do the business, for
he has always stuck by me." As for myself, the
Lord Jesus took me in as a poor prodigal son, and
it was not many weeks before He put me in trust
with the gospel, that greatest of all treasures ; this
was a grand love-token. I know of none to excel

it. The commission given to Peter proved how
thoroughly the breach was healed, how fully the
sin was forgiven, for Jesus took the man who had
cursed and sworn in denial of Him and bade him
feed His lambs and sheep. Oh, blessed work, not
for yourselves, and yet for yourselves! He that
serves himself shall lose himself, but he that loseth
himself doth really serve himself after the best
possible fashion.

The master-motive of a good shepherd is love.
We are to feed Christ's lambs *out of love*.

First, as a proof of love. "If ye love Me, keep
My commandments." If ye love Me, feed My
lambs. If ye love Christ, show it, and show it by
doing good to others, by laying yourself out to help
others, that Jesus may have joy of them.

Next, as an inflowing of love. "Feed My
lambs," for if you love Christ a little when you
begin to do good, you will soon love Him more.
Love grows by active exercise. It is like the
blacksmith's arm, which increases its strength by
wielding the hammer. Love loves till it loves
more, and it loves more till it loves more ; and it
still loves more till it loves most of all, and then
it is not satisfied, but aspires after enlargement of
heart that it may copy yet more fully the perfect
model of love in Christ Jesus, the Saviour.

Besides being an inflowing of love, the feeding of
lambs is an outflow of love. How often have we
told our Lord that we loved Him when we were
preaching, and I do not doubt you teachers feel
more of the pleasure of love to Jesus when you are

busy with your classes than when you are by yourselves at home. A person may go home and sit
down and groan out—

> "'Tis a point I long to know,
> Oft it causes anxious thought,"

and wipe his forehead and rub his eyes, and get
into the dumps without end ; but if he will rise up
and work for Jesus, the point he longs to know
will soon be settled, for love will come pouring out
of his heart till he can no longer question whether
it is there.

So let us abide in this blessed service for Christ
that it may be the delight of love, the very ocean
in which love shall swim, the sunlight in which it
shall bask. The recreation of a loving soul is
work for Jesus Christ ; and amongst the highest
and most delicious forms of this heavenly recreation
is the feeding of young Christians ; endeavouring
to build them up in knowledge and understanding,
that they may become strong in the Lord.

THE CHILD TIMOTHY AND HIS TEACHERS.

NOWADAYS, since the world has in it, alas! so few of Christian mothers and grandmothers, the church has thought it wise to supplement the instruction of home by teaching held under her fostering wing. Those children who have no such parents the church takes under her maternal care. I regard this as a very blessed institution. I am thankful for the many of our brothers and sisters who give their Sabbath-days, and many of them a considerable part of their week evenings also, to the teaching of other people's children, who somehow grow to be very much their own. They endeavour to perform the duties of fathers and mothers, for God's sake, to those children who are neglected by their own parents; and therein they do well. Let no Christian parents fall into the delusion that the Sunday-school is intended to ease them of their personal duties. The first and most natural condition of things is for Christian parents to train up their own children in the nurture and admonition of the Lord. Let holy grandmothers and gracious mothers, with their husbands, see to it that their own boys and girls are well taught in the Book of the Lord. Where there are no such Christian parents it is well and wisely done for godly people to intervene. It is a Christly work when others undertake the duty which the natural doers of it have left undone. The Lord Jesus looks with pleasure upon those who feed His lambs, and nurse His babes ; for it is not His will that any of these little ones should perish. Timothy had the great privilege of being taught by those whose natural duty it is ; but where that great privilege cannot be enjoyed, let us all, as God shall help us, try to make up to the children the terrible loss which they endure. Come forward, earnest men and women, and sanctify yourselves for this joyful service.

Note the subject of the instruction. " From a child thou hast known the holy Scriptures " : he was led to treat the book of God with great reverence. I lay stress upon that word " *holy* Scriptures." One of the first objects of the Sabbath-school should be to teach the children great reverence for these holy writings, these inspired Scriptures. The Jews esteemed the Old Testament beyond all price ; and though unfortunately many of them fell into a superstitious reverence for the letter and lost the spirit of it, yet were they much to be commended for their profound regard to the holy oracles. Especially is this feeling of reverence needed nowadays. I meet with men who hold strange views, but I do not care one-half so much about their views, nor about the strangeness of them, as I do

about a certain something which I spy out at the
back of this novel thinking. When I find that, if
I prove their views to be unscriptural, I have nevertheless proved nothing to them, for they do not
care about Scripture, then I have found out a principle far more dangerous than mere doctrinal
blundering. This indifference to Scripture is the
great curse of the church at this hour. We can be
tolerant of divergent opinions, so long as we perceive an honest intent to follow the Statute-book.
But if it comes to this, that the Book itself is of
small authority to you, then we have no need of
further parley : we are in different camps, and the
sooner we recognize this, the better for all parties
concerned. If we are to have a church of God at
all in the land, Scripture must be regarded as holy,
and to be had in reverence. This Scripture was
given by holy inspiration, and is not the result of
dim myths and dubious traditions ; neither has it
drifted down to us by the survival of the fittest as
one of the best of human books. It must be given
to our children, and accepted by ourselves, as the
infallible revelation of the Most Holy God. Lay
much stress upon this ; tell your children that the
Word of the Lord is a pure Word, as silver tried
in a furnace of earth, purified seven times. Let
their esteem for the Book of God be carried to the
highest point.

Observe that Timothy was taught, not only to
reverence holy things in general, but especially to
know the Scriptures. The teaching of his mother
and his grandmother was the teaching of holy

Scripture. Suppose we get the children together on Sabbath-days, and then amuse them and make the hours to pass away pleasantly ; or instruct them, as we do in the week-days, in the elements of a moral education, what have we done? We have done nothing worthy of the day, or of the church of God. Suppose that we are particularly careful to teach the children the rules and regulations of our own church, and do not take them to the Scriptures ; suppose that we bring before them a book which is set up as the standard of our church, but do not dwell upon the Bible—what have we done? The aforesaid standard may or may not be correct, and we may, therefore, have taught our children truth or have taught them error ; but if we keep to holy Scripture we cannot go aside. With such a standard we know that we are right. This Book is the Word of God, and if we teach it, we teach that which the Lord will accept and bless. O dear teachers—and I speak here to myself also—let our teaching be more and more Scriptural ! Fret not if our classes forget what *we* say, but pray them to remember what the Lord says. May Divine truths about sin, and righteousness, and judgment to come, be written on their hearts ! May revealed truths concerning the love of God, the grace of our Lord Jesus Christ, and the work of the Holy Ghost, never be forgotten by them ! May they know the virtue and necessity of the atoning blood of our Lord, the power of His resurrection, and the glory of His second coming ! May the doctrines of grace be graven as with a pen of iron upon their minds,

and written as with the point of a diamond upon
their hearts, never to be erased ! If we can
secure this, we have not lived in vain. The
generation now ruling seems bent on departing
from the eternal truth of God : but we shall not
despair if the gospel be impressed upon the memory
of the rising race.

Once more upon this point : it appears that young
Timothy was so taught as a child that the teaching
was effectual. " Thou hast *known* the holy Scriptures," says Paul. It is a good deal to say of a
child that he has " known the holy Scriptures." You
may say, "I have taught the children the Scriptures,"
but that they have known them is quite another
thing. Do all of you who are grown up know the
Scriptures ? I fear that although knowledge in
general increases, knowledge of the Scriptures is
far too rare. If we were now to hold an examination, I am afraid that some of you would hardly
shine in the lists at the end. But here was a little
child who knew the holy Scriptures : that is to
say, he had a remarkable acquaintance with them.
Children can get that : it is by no means an impossible attainment. God blessing your efforts,
dear friends, your children may know all of Scripture
that is necessary to their salvation. They may have
as true an idea of sin as their mother has ; they
may have as clear a view of the atonement as their
grandmother can have ; they may have as distinct
a faith in Jesus as any of us can have. The things
that make for our peace require no length of experience to prepare us for receiving them ; they are

among the simplicities of thought. He may run that readeth them ; and a child may read them as soon as he can run. The opinion that children cannot receive the whole truth of the gospel is a great mistake : for their child-condition is a help rather than a hindrance : older folk must become as little children before they can enter the kingdom. Do lay a good groundwork for the children. Let not Sunday-school work be slurred, nor done in a slovenly manner. Let the children know the holy Scriptures. Let the Scriptures be consulted rather than any human book.

This work was quickened by a saving faith. The Scriptures do not save, but they are able to make a man wise unto salvation. Children may know the Scriptures, and yet not be children of God. Faith in Jesus Christ is that grace which brings immediate salvation. Many dear children are called of God so early, that they cannot precisely tell when they were converted ; but they were converted : they must at some time or other have passed from death to life. You could not have told this morning, by observation, the moment when the sun rose, but it did rise ; and there was a time when it was below the horizon, and another time when it had risen above it. The moment, whether we see it or not, in which a child is really saved, is when he believes in the Lord Jesus Christ. Perhaps for years Lois and Eunice had been teaching the Old Testament to Timothy, while they themselves did not know the Lord Jesus ; and, if so, they were teaching him the type without the antitype—the riddles without the answers : but it was good teaching for all that, since it was all the truth which they then knew. How much happier, however, is our task, since we are able to teach concerning the Lord Jesus so plainly, having the New Testament to explain the Old ! May we not hope that even earlier in life than Timothy, our dear children may catch the thought that Christ Jesus is the sum and substance of holy Scripture, and so by faith in Him may receive power to become the sons of God ? I mention this, simple as it is, because I want all teachers to feel that if their children do not as yet know all the doctrines of the Bible, and if there be certain higher or deeper truths which their minds have not yet grasped, still children are saved as soon as they are wise unto salvation through faith which is in Christ Jesus. Faith in the Lord Jesus, as He is set forth in Scripture, will surely save. " If thou believest with all thine heart, thou mayest," said Philip to the eunuch ; and we say the same to every child : thou mayest confess thy faith if thou hast any true faith in Jesus to confess. If thou believest that Jesus is the Christ, and so dost put thy trust in Him, thou art as truly saved as though grey hairs adorned thy brow.

By this faith in Christ Jesus we continue and advance in salvation. The moment we believe in Christ, we are saved ; but we are not at once as wise as we may be, and hope to be. We may be, as it were, saved unintelligently—I mean, of course, comparatively so ; but it is desirable that we should be able to give a reason for the hope that is in us, and so be wise unto salvation. By faith children become little disciples, and by faith they go on to become more proficient. How are we to go on to wisdom? Not by quitting the way of faith, but by keeping to that same faith in Christ Jesus by which we began to learn. In the school of grace faith is the great faculty by which we make advances in wisdom. If by faith thou hast been able to say A and B and C, it must be by faith that thou shalt go on to say D and E and F, until thou shalt come to the end of the alphabet, and be an expert in the Book of Wisdom. If by faith thou canst read in the spelling-book of simple faith, by the same faith in Christ Jesus thou must go on to read in the classics of full assurance, and become a scribe well instructed in the things of the kingdom. Keep therefore close to the practice of faith, from which so many are turning aside. In these times men look to make progress by what they call *thought*, by which they mean vain imagination and speculation. We cannot advance a step by doubt; our only progress is by faith. There are no such things as "stepping-stones of our dead selves"; unless, indeed, they be stepping-stones down to death and destruction; the only stepping-stones to life and heaven are to be found in the truth of God revealed to our faith. Believe God, and thou hast made progress. So let us pray for our children, that constantly they may know and believe more and more; for the Scripture is able to make them wise unto salvation, but only through faith which is in Christ Jesus. Faith is the result to aim at; faith

5

in the appointed, anointed, and exalted Saviour. This is the anchorage to which we would bring these little ships, for here they will abide in perfect safety.

Sound instruction in holy Scripture, when quickened by a living faith, creates a solid character. The man who from a child has known the holy Scriptures, when he obtains faith in Christ will be grounded and settled upon the abiding principles of the unchanging Word of God.

O teachers, see what you may do! In your schools sit our future Evangelists. In that infant class sits an apostle to some distant land. There may come under your training hand, my sister, a future father in Israel. There shall come under your teaching, my brother, those who are to bear the banners of the Lord in the thick of the fray. The ages look to you each time your class assembles. Oh, that God may help you to do your part well! We pray with one heart and one soul that the Lord Jesus Christ may be with our Sunday-schools from this day and till He cometh.

"WHAT MEAN YE BY THIS SERVICE?" *

WE should view everything in this world by the light of redemption, and then we shall view it aright. It makes a wonderful change whether you view Providence from the standpoint of human merit or from the foot of the cross. We see nothing truly till Jesus is our light. Everything is seen in its reality when you look through the glass, the ruby glass of the atoning sacrifice. Use this telescope of the cross, and you shall see far and clear ; look at sinners through the cross ; look at saints through the cross ; look at sin through the cross ; look at the world's joys and sorrows through the cross ; look at heaven and hell through the cross. See how conspicuous the blood of the Passover was meant to be, and then learn from all this to make much of the sacrifice of Jesus —yea, to make everything of it, for Christ is all.

We read in Deuteronomy, in the sixth chapter, and the eighth verse, concerning the commandments of the Lord, as follows : "And thou shalt

---

* Exodus xii.

bind them for a sign upon thine hand, and they
shall be as frontlets between thine eyes. And thou
shalt write them upon the posts of thy house, and
on thy gates." See, then, that the law is to be
written hard by the memorials of the blood. In
Switzerland, in the Protestant villages, you have
seen texts of Scripture upon the doorposts. I half
wish we had that custom in England. How much
of gospel might be preached to wayfarers if texts
of Scripture were over Christian people's doors!
It might be ridiculed as Pharisaical, but we could
get over that. Few are liable to that charge in
these days through being religious overmuch. I
like to see texts of Scripture in our houses, in all
the rooms, on the cornices, and on the walls; but
outside on the door—what a capital advertisement
the gospel might get at a cheap rate! But note,
that when the Jew wrote upon his doorposts a
promise, or a precept, or a doctrine, he had to
write upon a surface stained with blood, and when
the next year's Passover came round he had to
sprinkle the blood with the hyssop right over the
writing. It seems to me so delightful to think of
the law of God in connection with that atoning
sacrifice, which has magnified it and made it
honourable. God's commands come to me as a
redeemed man; his promises are to me as a blood-
bought man; his teaching instructs me as one for
whom atonement has been made. The law in the
hand of Christ is not a sword to slay us, but a
jewel to enrich us. All truth taken in connection
with the cross is greatly enhanced in value. Holy

Scripture itself becomes dear to a sevenfold degree
when we see that it comes to us as the redeemed
of the Lord, and bears upon its every page marks
of those dear hands which were nailed to the tree
for us.

You now see how everything was done that
could well be thought of to bring the blood of the
Paschal lamb into a high position in the esteem of
the people whom the Lord brought out of Egypt ;
and you and I must do everything we can think of
to bring forward, and keep before men for ever, the
precious doctrine of the atoning sacrifice of Christ.
He was made sin for us though He knew no sin,
that we might be made the righteousness of God
in Him.

And now I will remind you of the institution
that was connected with the remembrance of the
Passover. "It shall come to pass, when your
children shall say unto you, What mean ye by this
service ? that ye shall say, It is the sacrifice of the
Lord's Passover."

Inquiry should be excited in the minds of our
children. Oh, that we could get them to ask
questions about the things of God ! Some of them
enquire very early, others of them seem diseased
with much the same indifference as older folks.
With both orders of mind we have to deal. It is
well to explain to children the ordinance of the
Lord's Supper, for this shows forth the death of
Christ in symbol. I regret that children do not
oftener see this ordinance. Baptism and the Lord's
Supper should both be placed in view of the rising

generation, that they may then ask us, "What mean ye by this?" Now, the Lord's Supper is a perennial gospel sermon, and it turns mainly upon the sacrifice for sin. You may banish the doctrine of the atonement from the pulpit, but it will always live in the church through the Lord's Supper. You cannot explain that broken bread and that cup filled with the fruit of the vine, without reference to our Lord's atoning death. You cannot explain "the communion of the body of Christ" without bringing in, in some form or other, the death of Jesus in our place and stead. Let your little ones, then, see the Lord's Supper, and let them be told most clearly what it sets forth. And if not the Lord's Supper—for that is not the thing itself, but only the shadow of the glorious fact—dwell much and often in their presence upon the sufferings and death of our Redeemer Let them think of Gethsemane, and Gabbatha, and Golgotha, and let them learn to sing in plaintive tones of Him who laid down His life for us. Tell them who it was that suffered, and why. Yes, though the hymn is hardly to my taste in some of its expressions, I would have the children sing—

> "There is a green hill far away,
>   Without a city wall."

And I would have them learn such lines as these :

> " He knew how wicked we had been,
>   And knew that God must punish sin ;
>   So out of pity Jesus said,
>   He'd bear the punishment instead."

And when attention is excited upon the best of

themes, let us be ready to explain the great trans-
action by which God is just, and yet sinners are
justified. Children can well understand the doctrine
of the expiatory sacrifice ; it was meant to be a
gospel for the youngest. The gospel of substitution
is a simplicity, though it is a mystery. We ought
not to be content until our little ones know and
trust in their finished Sacrifice. This is essential
knowledge, and the key to all other spiritual
teaching. May our dear children know the cross,
and they will have begun well. With all their
gettings may they get an understanding of this,
and they will have the foundation rightly laid.

This will necessitate your teaching the child his
need of a Saviour. You must not hold back from
this needful task. Do not flatter the child with
delusive rubbish about his nature being good and
needing to be developed. Tell him he must be
born again. Don't bolster him up with the fancy
of his own innocence, but show him his sin.
Mention the childish sins to which he is prone, and
pray the Holy Spirit to work conviction in his
heart and conscience. Deal with the young in
much the same way as you would with the old.
Be thorough and honest with them. Flimsy
religion is neither good for young nor old. These
boys and girls need pardon through the precious
blood as surely as any of us. Do not hesitate to
tell the child his ruin ; he will not else desire the
remedy. Tell him also of the punishment of sin,
and warn him of its terror. Be tender, but be true.
Do not hide from the youthful sinner the truth,

however terrible it may be. Now that he has come to years of responsibility, if he believes not in Christ, it will go ill with him at the last great day. Set before him the judgment-seat, and remind him that he will have to give an account of things done in the body. Labour to arouse the conscience ; and pray God the Holy Spirit to work by you till the heart becomes tender and the mind perceives the need of the great salvation.

Children need to learn the doctrine of the cross that they may find immediate salvation. I thank God that in our Sabbath-school we believe in the salvation of children as children. How very many has it been my joy to see of boys and girls who have come forward to confess their faith in Christ ! And I again wish to say that the best converts, the clearest converts, the most intelligent converts we have ever had have been the young ones ; and, instead of there being any deficiency in their knowledge of the Word of God, and the doctrines of grace, we have usually found them to have a very delightful acquaintance with the great cardinal truths of Christ. Many of these dear children have been able to speak of the things of God with great pleasure of heart and force of understanding. Go on, dear teachers, and believe that God will save your children. Be not content to sow principles in their minds which may possibly develop in after years, but be working for immediate conversion. Expect fruit in your children while they are children. Pray for them that they may not run into the world and fall into the evils of outward sin, and then come back with broken bones to the Good Shepherd ; but that they may by God's rich grace be kept from the paths of the destroyer, and grow up in the fold of Christ, first as lambs of His flock, and then as sheep of His hand.

One thing I am sure of, and that is, that if we teach the children the doctrine of the atonement in the most unmistakable terms, we shall be doing ourselves good. I sometimes hope that God will revive His church and restore her to her ancient faith by a gracious work among children. If He would bring into our churches a large influx of young people, how it would tend to quicken the sluggish blood of the supine and sleepy ! Child Christians tend to keep the house alive. Oh, for more of them ! If the Lord will but help us to teach the children we shall be teaching ourselves. There is no way of learning like teaching, and you do not know a thing till you can teach it to another. You do not thoroughly know any truth till you can put it before a child so that he can see it. In trying to make a little child understand the doctrine of the atonement you will get clearer views of it yourselves, and therefore I commend the holy exercise to you.

What a mercy it will be if our children are thoroughly grounded in the doctrine of redemption by Christ ! If they are warned against the false gospels of this evil age, and if they are taught to rest on the eternal rock of Christ's finished work, we may hope to have a generation following us which will maintain the faith, and will be better than their fathers. Your Sunday-schools are admirable ; but what is their purpose if you do not teach the gospel in them ? You get children together and keep them quiet for an hour-and-a-half, and then send them home ; but what is the good of it ? It may bring some quiet to their fathers and mothers, and that is, perhaps, why they send them to the school ; but all the real good lies in what is taught the children. The most fundamental truth should be made most prominent; and what is this but the cross. Some talk to children about being good boys and girls, and so on ; that is to say, they preach the law to the children, though they would preach the gospel to grown-up people. Is this honest ? Is this wise ? Children need the gospel, the whole gospel, the unadulterated gospel ; they ought to have it, and if they are taught of the Spirit of God they are as capable of receiving it as persons of ripe years. Teach the little ones that Jesus died, the just for the unjust, to bring us to God. Very, very confidently do I leave this work in the hands of teachers. I never knew a nobler body of Christian men and women ; for they are as earnest in their attachment to the Old Gospel as they are eager for the winning of souls. Be encouraged ; the God who has saved so many of your children is going to save very many more of them, and we shall have great joy as we see hundreds brought to Christ.

SAMUEL AND HIS TEACHERS.

N the days of Eli the word of the Lord was precious, and there was no open vision. It was well when the word did come, that one chosen individual had the hearing ear to receive it, and the obedient heart to perform it. Eli failed to tutor his sons to be the willing servants and the attentive hearers of the Lord's word. In this he was without the excuse of inability, since he successfully trained the child Samuel in reverent attention to the Divine will. O that those who are diligent about the souls of others, would look well to their own households. Alas, poor Eli, like many in our day, they made thee keeper of the vineyards, but thine own vineyard thou hast not kept. As often as he looked upon the gracious child, Samuel, he must have felt the heart-ache. When he remembered his own neglected and unchastened sons, and how they had made themselves vile before all Israel, Samuel was the living witness of what grace can work where children are trained up in God's fear, and Hophni and

Phineas were sad specimens of what parental in-
dulgence will produce in the children of the best of
men.   Ah, Eli, if thou hadst been as careful with
thine own sons as with the son of Hannah, they had
not been such men of Belial, nor would Israel have
abhorred the offering of the Lord because of the
fornication which those priestly reprobates committed at the very door of the tabernacle.   O for
grace so to nurse our little ones for the Lord, that
they may hear the Lord when He shall be pleased
to speak unto them.

Samuel was blessed with a gracious father, and
what is of even more importance, he was the child
of an eminently holy mother.   Hannah was a
woman of great poetic talent, as appears from her
memorable song—" My heart rejoiceth in the Lord,
mine horn is exalted in the Lord ; my mouth is
enlarged over mine enemies, because I rejoiced in
Thy salvation."   The soul of poetry lives in every
line ; a brave but chastened spirit breathes in every
sentence ; even the Virgin Mary, the most blessed
among women, could do no other than use expressions of a similar import.   Better still, Hannah was
a woman of great prayer.   She had been a woman
of a sorrowful spirit, but her prayers at last returned
to her in blessing, and she had this son given her
of the Lord.   He was very dear to his mother's
heart, and she, therefore, to show her gratitude,
and in fulfilment of the vow which in her anguish
she had vowed unto the Lord, would consecrate
the best thing she had, and presented her son before
the Lord in Shiloh—a lesson to all godly parents,

to see to it that they dedicate their children unto God. How highly favoured shall we be if our children shall all be like Isaac—children of the promise! What blessed parents should we be if we saw our children all rise up to call the Redeemer blessed! It has been the lot of some of you to see all your children numbered with the people of God : all your jewels are now in Jehovah's casket. In their early childhood you gave them up to God, and dedicated them to Him in earnest prayer, and now the Lord has given you your petition which you asked of Him. I like our friends to hold little services in their own houses when their family is increased ; it seems good and profitable for friends to assemble, and prayer to be offered that the child may be an inheritor of the promises, that he may be early called by mighty grace, and received into the Divine family. You will perceive that as Samuel was put under the care and tuition of Eli, Eli had instructed him in some degree in the spirit of religion, but he does not appear to have explained to him the peculiar form and nature of those special and particular manifestations of God which were given to His prophets ; little dreaming, I dare say, that Samuel would ever be himself the subject of them. On that memorable night, when towards morning the lamp of God was about to go out, the Lord cried, " Samuel, Samuel," the young child was not able to discern—for he had not been taught— that it was the voice of God, and not the voice of man. That he had learned the spirit of true religion, is indicated by his instantaneous obedience, and the habit of obedience became a valuable guide to him in the perplexities of that eventful hour. He runs to Eli, and says, " Here am I, for thou didst call me ; " and though this is three times repeated, yet he seemed nothing loath to leave his warm bed, and run to his foster-father, to see if he could get him any comfort that his old age might require during the night, or otherwise do his bidding—a sure sign that the child had acquired the healthy principle of obedience, though he did not understand the mystery of the prophetic call. Better far to have the young heart trained to bear the yoke than to fill the childish head with knowledge, however valuable. An ounce of obedience is better than a ton of learning.

When Eli perceived that God had called the child, he taught him his first little prayer. It is a very short one, but it is a very full one—" Speak, Lord ; for Thy servant heareth." Let the Christian parent explain to the child what prayer is ; tell him that God answers prayer ; direct him to the Saviour, and then urge him to express his desires in his own language, both when he rises, and when he goes to rest. Gather the little ones around your knee and listen to their words, suggesting to them their needs, and reminding them of God's gracious promise. You will be amazed, and, I may add, sometimes amused too ; but you will be frequently surprised at the expressions they will use, the confessions they will make, the desires they will utter ; and I am certain that any Christian person standing within ear-shot, and listening to the simple prayer of a little child earnestly asking God for what it thinks it wants, would never afterwards wish to teach a child a form, but would say that as a matter of education to the heart the extemporaneous utterance was infinitely superior to the best form, and that the form should be given up for ever. However, do not let me speak too sweepingly. If you must teach your child to say a form of prayer, at least take care that you do not teach him to say anything which is not true. If you teach your children a catechism, mind that it is thoroughly scriptural, or you may train them up to tell falsehoods. Teach him nothing but the truth as it is in Jesus so far as he can learn it, and pray the Holy Spirit to write that truth upon his heart. Better to supply no sign-posts to the young traveller than to mislead him with false ones. The light of a wrecker's beacon is worse than darkness. Teach our youth to make untruthful statements in religious matters, and Atheism can scarcely do more to corrupt their minds. Formal religion is a deadly foe to vital godliness. If you teach a catechism, or if you teach a form of prayer to your little ones, let it be all true ; and, as far as possible, never put into a child's mouth a word which the child cannot truly say from his heart.

We must be more careful about truthfulness and correctness in speech. If a child looked out of a window at anything going on in the street, and then told you that he saw it from the door, you ought to make him tell the tale over again, so as to impress upon him the necessity of being truthful in every respect. Especially in things connected with religion, keep your child back from any form until he has a right to be a partaker of it. Never encourage him to come to the Lord's Table unless you really believe that there is a work of grace in his heart; for why should you lead him to eat and drink his own damnation? Insist with all your heart that religion is a solemn reality not to be mimicked or pretended to, and seek to bring the child to understand that there is no vice more abhorrent before God than hypocrisy. Do not make your young Samuel a young hypocrite, but train up your darling to speak before the Lord with a deep solemnity and a conscientious truthfulness, and let him never dare to say, either in answer to a catechismal question, or as a form of prayer, anything which is not positively true. If you must have a form of prayer, let it not express such desires as a child never had, but let it be adapted to his young capacity.

It is said of the Rev. John Angell James, " Like most men who have been eminent and honoured in the Church of Christ, he had a godly mother, who was wont to take her children to her chamber, and with each separately to pray for the salvation of their souls. This exercise, which fulfilled her own responsibility, was moulding the character of her children, and most, if not all of them, rose up to call her blessed. When did such means ever fail?" I beseech you, the teachers of the Sunday-school—though I scarcely need to do so, for I know how zealous you are in this matter—as soon as ever you see the first peep of day in your children, encourage their young desires. Believe in the conversion of children, as children ; believe that the Lord can call them by His grace, can renew their hearts, can give them a part and a lot among His people long before they reach the prime of life.

INSTRUCTIONS FOR TEACHERS
AND PARENTS.

IRST, get the children to come to your school. The great complaint with some teachers is, that they cannot obtain scholars. In London, we are having a canvass of the children ; that is a good idea, and you ought to have a canvass of every country village, and of every market-town, and get into the Sunday-school every child you can. My advice to you is, get the children to come by all fair and right means. Do not bribe them ; that is a plan to which we strongly object, and it is only adopted in schools of the lowest order, schools of so mean a class that even the fathers and mothers of the children have too much sense to send them there. " But, then, Farmer Brown won't employ them, or the squire will turn them out of their situations ; or, if the children don't go to the school on Sundays, they shall not go on week-days." Oh, that beggarly trick of bribing ! I wish there were an end of it ; it only shows the weakness, and degradation, and abomination of a sect that cannot succeed without using so mean a system. But with the exception of that method, do not be very particular how you get the children to school. Why, if I could not get people to come to my chapel by preaching in a black coat, I would have regimentals to-morrow, I would have a congregation somehow. Better do strange things than have an empty chapel, or an empty schoolroom. When I was in Scotland, we sent a bellman round a village to secure an audience, and the plan was eminently successful. Spare no right means, but do get the children in. I have known ministers who have gone out into the streets on the Lord's-day afternoon, and talked to the children who were playing about, and so induced them to come to the school. This is what an earnest teacher will do ; he will say, " John, come into our school ; you cannot think what a nice place it is." Then he gets the children in, and in his kind, winning manner he tells them stories and anecdotes about girls and boys who loved the Saviour, and in this way the school is filled. Go and catch the children. There is no law against it ; all is fair in war against the devil. So my first instruction is, get the children, and get them anyhow that you can.

Next, get the children to love you, if you can. " Come, ye children, hearken unto me." You know how we used to be taught in the dame's school, how we stood up with our hands behind us to repeat our lessons. That was not David's plan. " Come, ye children,—come here, and sit on my knee." " Oh ! " thinks the child, " how nice to

have such a teacher, a teacher who will let me
come near him, a teacher who does not say, 'Go,'
but 'Come!'" The fault of many teachers is that
they do not get their children near them; but
endeavour to foster in their scholars a kind of
awful respect. Before you can teach children, you
must get the silver key of kindness to unlock their
hearts, and so secure their attention. Say, "Come,
ye children." We have known some good men
who were objects of abhorrence to children. You
remember the story of two little boys who were
one day asked if they would like to go to Heaven,
and who, much to their teacher's astonishment,
said that they really should not. When they were
asked, "Why not?" one of them said, "I should
not like to go to Heaven because grandpa would
be there, and he would be sure to say, 'Get along,
boys; be off with you!' I should not like to be
in Heaven with grandpa." So, if a boy has a
teacher who talks to him about Jesus, but who
always wears a sour look, what does the boy think?
"I wonder whether Jesus is like you; if so, I
shouldn't like Him." Then there is another
teacher, who, if he is provoked ever so little, boxes
the child's ears; and, at the same time, teaches
him that he should forgive others, and be kind to
them. "Well," thinks the lad, "that is very pretty,
no doubt, but my teacher doesn't show me how to
do it." If you drive a boy from you, your power
over him is gone, for you will not be able to teach
him anything. It is of no avail to attempt teaching
those who do not love you; so, try and make them

love you, and then they will learn anything from you.

Next, get the children's attention. " Come, ye children, hearken unto me." If they do not *hearken*, you may talk, but you will speak to no purpose whatever. If they do not listen, you go through your labour as an unmeaning drudgery to yourselves and to your scholars, too. You can do nothing without securing their attention. "That is just what I cannot do," says one. Well, that depends upon yourself ; if you give them something worth attending to, they will be sure to attend. Give them something worth hearing, and they will certainly hearken. This rule may not be universal, but it is very nearly so. Don't forget to give them a few anecdotes. Anecdotes are very much objected to by critics of sermons, who say they ought not to be used in the pulpit ; but some of us know better than that, we know what will wake a congregation up ; we can testify, from experience, that a few anecdotes here and there are first-rate things to get the attention of persons who will not listen to dry doctrine. Do try and gather as many good illustrations in the week as you possibly can ; wherever you go, if you are really a wise teacher, you can always find something to make into a tale to tell your children. Then, when your scholars get dull, and you are losing their attention, say to them, " Do you know the Five Bells ? " If there is such a place in the village, they all open their eyes directly ; or you ask, " Do know the turning against the Red Lion ? "

Then tell them something you have read or heard which will secure their attention to the lesson. A dear child once said, "Father, I like to hear Mr. So-and-so preach, because he puts so many ' likes' into his sermon ; —' like this, and like that.' " Yes, children always love those *likes."* Make parables, pictures, figures for them, and you will always get on. I am sure, if I were a boy listening to some of you, unless you told me a tale now and then, you would as often see the back of my head as my face ; and I do not know, if I sat in a hot school-room, but that my head would nod, and I should go to sleep, or be playing with Tom on my left, and do as many strange things as the rest, if you did not strive to interest me. Remember, then, to make your scholars " hearken."

A MODEL LESSON FOR TEACHERS.

TEACH them *morality :* " Keep thy tongue from evil, and thy lips from speaking guile. Depart from evil, and do good ; seek peace, and pursue it." Now, we never teach morality as the way of salvation. God forbid that we should ever mix up man's works in any way with the redemption which is in Christ Jesus ! " By grace are ye saved through faith, and that not of yourselves, it is the gift of God." Yet we teach morality while we teach spirituality ; and I have always found that the gospel produces the best morality in all the world. I would have a Sunday-school teacher watchful over the morals of the boys and girls under his care, speaking to them very particularly of those sins which are most common to youth. He may honestly and conveniently say many things to his children which no one else can say, especially when reminding them of the sin of lying, so common with children, or the sin of petty theft, or of disobedience to parents, or of breaking the Sabbath-day. I would have the teacher be very particular in mentioning these evils one by one ; for it is of little avail talking to them about sins in the mass, you must take them one by one, just as David did. First look after *the tongue :* " Keep thy tongue from evil, and thy lips from speaking guile." Then look after *the whole conduct :* " Depart from evil, and do good ; seek peace, and pursue it." If the child's soul is not saved by other parts of the teaching, this part may have a beneficial effect upon his life, and so far so good. Morality, however, by itself is comparatively a small thing. The best part of what you teach is *godliness.* I said not, "*religion*," but *godliness.* Many people are *religious* after a fashion, without being godly. Many have all the externals of godliness, all the outside of piety ; such men we call " religious," but they have no right thought about God. They think about their place of worship, their Sunday, their books, but nothing about God. He who does not respect God, pray to God, love God, is an ungodly man, whatever his external religion may be. Labour to teach the child always to have an eye to God ; write on his memory these words, " Thou God seest me." Bid him remember that his every act and thought are under the eye of God. No Sunday-school teacher discharges his duty unless he constantly lays stress upon the fact that there is a God who notices everything that happens. Oh, that we were more godly ourselves; that we talked more of godliness, and that we loved godliness better !

The third lesson is, *the evil of sin.* If the child does not learn *that*, he will never learn the way to

Heaven. None of us ever knew what a Saviour Christ was till we knew what an evil thing sin was. If the Holy Ghost does not teach us the exceeding sinfulness of sin, we shall never know the blessedness of salvation. Let us seek His grace, then, when we teach, that we may always be able to lay stress upon the abominable nature of sin. "The face of the Lord is against them that do evil, to cut off the remembrance of them from the earth." Do not spare your child ; let him know what sin leads to. Do not, like some people, be afraid of speaking plainly and broadly concerning the consequences of sin. I have heard of a father, one of whose sons, a very ungodly young man, was taken off in a very sudden manner. The father did not, as some would have done, say to his family, "We hope your brother has gone to Heaven." No ; but overcoming his natural feelings, he was enabled, by Divine grace, to assemble his children together, and to say to them, "My sons and daughters, your brother is dead ; I fear he is in hell. You knew his life and conduct, you saw how he behaved ; and now God has snatched him away in his sins." Then he solemnly told them of the place of woe to which he believed—yea, almost knew he was gone, begging them to shun it, and to flee from the wrath to come. Thus he was the means of bringing his children to serious thought ; but had he acted, as some would have done, with tenderness of heart, but not with honesty of purpose, and said he hoped his son had gone to Heaven, what would the other children have said ? "If he is gone to

Heaven, there is no need for us to fear; we may live as we like." No, no; I hold that it is not unchristian to say of some men that they are gone to hell, when we have seen that their lives have been hellish lives. But it is asked, " Can you judge your fellow-creatures?" No, but I can *know* them by their fruits. I do not judge them, or condemn them; they judge themselves. I have seen their sins go beforehand to judgment, and I do not doubt that they shall follow after. " But may they not be saved at the eleventh hour?" I have heard of *one* who was, but I do not know that there ever was another, and I cannot tell that there ever will be. Be honest, then, with your children, and teach them, by the help of God, that " evil shall slay the wicked."

But you will not have done half enough unless you teach carefully the fourth lesson,—the absolute necessity of a change of heart. " The Lord is nigh unto them that are of a broken heart; and saveth such as be of a contrite spirit." Oh! may God enable us to keep this constantly before the minds of the taught, that there must be a broken heart and a contrite spirit, that good works will be of no avail unless there be a new nature, that the most arduous duties and the most earnest prayers will all be as nothing, unless there be a true and thorough repentance for sin, and an entire forsaking of sin through the grace and mercy of God! Be sure, whatever you leave out, that you teach the children the three R's,— Ruin, Redemption, and Regeneration. Tell the children they are *ruined* by the Fall, and that there is salvation for them only by being *redeemed* by the blood of Jesus Christ, and *regenerated* by the Holy Spirit. Keep constantly before them these vital truths, and then you will have the pleasing task of telling them the sweet subject of the closing lesson.

In the fifth place, tell the children of the joy and blessedness of being Christians. "The Lord redeemeth the soul of His servants : and none of them that trust in Him shall be desolate." I need not tell you how to talk about that theme ; for if you know what it is to be a Christian, you will never be short of matter. When we get on this subject, our mind cares not to speak ; it would rather revel in its bliss. Truly was it said, "Blessed is he whose transgression is forgiven, whose sin is covered." "Blessed is that man that maketh the Lord his trust." Yea, verily, blessed is the man, the woman, the child that trusteth in the Lord Jesus Christ, and whose hope is in Him. Always lay a stress upon this point,—that the righteous are a blessed people, that the chosen family of God, redeemed by blood and saved by power, are a blessed people while here below, and that they will be a blessed people for ever in Heaven above. Let your children see that you belong to that blessed company. If they know you are in trouble, if it be possible, come to your class with a smiling face, so that your scholars may be able to say : "Teacher is a blessed man, although he is bowed down by his troubles." Always seek to keep a joyous face, that your boys

and girls may know that your religion is a blessed
reality.   Let this be one main point of your
teaching, that though "many are the afflictions of
the righteous," yet "the Lord delivereth him out
of them all.   He keepeth all his bones : not one of
them is broken. . . . . The Lord redeemeth the soul
of His servants : and none of them that trust in
Him shall be desolate"

Thus have I given you five lessons ; and now let
me solemnly say that, with all the instruction you
may give to your children, you must all of you be
deeply conscious that you are not capable of doing
anything in the securing of the child's salvation,
but that it is God Himself who, from the first to
the last, must effect it all.   You are simply a pen ;
God can write with you, but you cannot write anything of yourself.   You are a sword ; God can with
you slay the child's sin, but you cannot slay it of
yourself.   Be ye, therefore, always mindful of this,
that you must be first taught of God yourself, and
then you must ask God to use you to teach ; for
unless a higher Teacher than you work with you,
and instruct the child, the child must perish.   It is
not your instruction that can save the souls of your
children ; it is the blessing of God the Holy Spirit
accompanying your labours.   May God bless and
crown your efforts with abundant success !   He
will surely do so if you are instant in prayer,
constant in supplication.   Never yet did the earnest
teacher or preacher "labour in vain in the Lord,"
and often has it been seen that bread cast upon the
waters has been found after many days.

"COME, YE CHILDREN."—THREE ADMONITIONS.

FIRST, recollect whom you are teaching; "Come, ye children." I think we ought always to have respect to our audience; I do not mean that we need care if we are preaching to Mr. So-and-so, Sir William this, or My Lord that,—because in God's sight such titles are the merest trifles; but we are to remember that we are preaching to men and women who have souls, so that we ought not to occupy their time by things that are not worth their hearing. But when you teach in Sabbath-schools, you are, if it be possible, in a more responsible situation even than a minister occupies. He preaches to grown-up people, to men of judgment, who, if they do not like what he preaches, can go somewhere else; but you teach children who have no option of going elsewhere. If you teach the child wrongly, he believes you; if you teach him heresies, he will receive them; what you teach him now, he will never forget. You are not sowing, as some say, on virgin soil, for it has long been occupied by the devil; but you are sowing on a soil more fertile now than it ever will be again, —soil that will produce fruit now, far better than it will do in after days; you are sowing on a young heart, and what you sow will be pretty sure to abide there, especially if you teach evil, for that will never be forgotten. You are beginning with the child; take care what you do with him. Do not spoil him. Many a child has been treated like the Indian children who have copper plates put upon their foreheads, so that they may never grow. There are many who are simpletons now, just because those who had the care of them when young gave them no opportunities of getting knowledge, so that, when they became old, they cared nothing about it. Have a care what you are after; you are teaching children, mind what you teach them. Put poison in the spring, and it will pollute the whole stream. Take care what you are after! You are twisting the sapling, and the old oak will be bent thereby. Have a care, it is a child's soul you are tampering with, if you are tampering at all; it is a child's soul you are preparing for eternity, if God is with you. I give you a solemn admonition on every child's behalf. Surely, if it be murder to administer poison to the dying, it must be far more criminal to give poison to the young life. If it be evil to mislead grey-headed age, it must be far more so to turn aside the feet of the young into the road of error, in which they may for ever walk.

Second, recollect that you are teaching for God.

"Come, ye children, hearken unto me ; I will teach you the fear of the Lord." If you, as teachers, were only assembled to teach geography, it might not injure them eternally if you were to tell the children that the North Pole was close to the Equator ; or if you were to say that the extremity of South America was hard by the coast of Europe ; or if you assured them that England was in the middle of Africa. But you are not teaching geography, or astronomy, nor are you training the children for a business life in this world ; but you are, to the best of your ability, teaching them for God. You say to them, "Children, you come here to be taught the Word of God ; you come here, if it be possible, that we may be the means of the salvation of your souls." Have a care what you are after when you pretend to be teaching them for God. Wound the child's hand if you will ; but, for God's sake, do not wound his heart. Say what you like about temporal things ; but, I beseech you, in spiritual matters, take care how you lead him. Be careful that it is the truth which you inculcate, and only that. With such a responsibility, how solemn your work becomes ! He who is doing a work for himself, may do it as he likes ; but he who is labouring for another, must take care to please his master ; he who is employed by a monarch must beware how he performs his duty ; but he who labours for God must tremble lest he doth his work ill. Remember that you are labouring for God, if you are what you profess to be. Alas ! many, I fear, are far from having this serious view of the work of a Sunday-school teacher.

Third, remember that your children need teaching. "Come, ye children, hearken unto me : I will teach you the fear of the Lord." That makes your work all the more solemn. If children did not need teaching, I would not be so extremely anxious that you should teach them aright. Works of supererogation, works that are not necessary, men may do as they please ; but this work is absolutely necessary. Your child needs teaching. He was born in iniquity ; in sin did his mother conceive him. He has an evil heart ; he knows not God, and he never will know the Lord unless he is taught. He is not like some ground of which we have heard, that hath good seed lying hidden in its very bowels ; but, instead thereof, he hath evil seed within his heart. God can place good seed there. You profess to be His instruments to scatter seed upon that child's heart ; remember, if that seed be not sown, he will be lost for ever, his life will be a life of alienation from God ; and at his death everlasting punishment must be his portion. Be careful, then, how you teach, re-membering the urgent necessity of the case. This is not a house on fire, needing your assistance at the engine ; nor is it a wreck at sea, demanding your oar in the lifeboat ; but it is a deathless spirit calling aloud to you, " Come and help me." There-fore, I beseech you, teach the fear of the Lord, and that only ; be very anxious to say, and to say truly, " I will teach you the fear of the Lord."

"COME, YE CHILDREN"—
THE PSALMIST'S INVITATION.*

IT is a singular thing that good men frequently discover their duty when they are placed in most humiliating positions. Never in David's life was he in a worse plight than that which suggested this Psalm. It is headed, "A Psalm of David, when he changed his behaviour before Abimelech; who drove him away, and he departed." This poem was intended to commemorate that event, and was suggested by it. David was carried before King Achish, the Abimelech of Philistia, and, in order to make his escape, he pretended to be mad, accompanying that profession of madness with certain very degrading actions which might well seem to betoken his insanity. He was driven from the palace, and as usual, when such men are in the street, it is probable that a number of children assembled around him. You have the sad story told in 1 Samuel xxi. 10—15. In after days, when David sang songs of praise to

---

* Psalm xxxiv. 11.

Jehovah, recollecting how he had become the laugh-
ing-stock of little children, he seemed to say, "Ah!
by my folly before the children in the streets, I have
lowered myself in the estimation of generations
that shall live after me ; now I will endeavour to
undo the mischief,—' Come, ye children, hearken
unto me : I will teach you the fear of the Lord.'"

Very possibly, if David had never been in such
a position, he would never have thought of this
duty; for I do not discover that he ever said in any
other Psalm, " Come, ye children, hearken unto
me." He had the cares of his cities, his provinces,
and his nation pressing upon him, and he may have
been at other times but little attentive to the education of youth ; but here, being brought into the
meanest position which man could possibly occupy,
having become as one bereft of reason, he recollects
his duty. The exalted or prosperous Christian is
not always mindful of "the lambs." That duty
generally devolves on Peters, whose pride and confidence have been crushed, and who rejoice thus
practically to answer their Lord's question, as the
apostle did when Jesus said to him, " Lovest thou
Me?"

" Come, ye children, hearken unto me : I will
teach you the fear of the Lord." The doctrine is,
that children are capable of being taught the fear
of the Lord.

Men are generally wisest after they have been
most foolish. David had been extremely foolish,
and now he became truly wise ; and being so, it
was not likely he would utter foolish sentiments, or

give directions such as would be dictated by a weak mind. We have heard it said by some that children cannot understand the great mysteries of religion. We even know some Sunday-school teachers who cautiously avoid mentioning the great doctrines of the gospel, because they think the children are not prepared to receive them. Alas! the same mistake has crept into the pulpit; for it is currently believed, among a certain class of preachers, that many of the doctrines of the Word of God, although true, are not fit to be taught to the people, since they would pervert them to their own destruction. Away with such priestcraft! Whatever God has revealed ought to be preached. Whatever HE has revealed, if I am not capable of understanding it, I will still believe and preach it. I do hold that there is no doctrine of the Word of God which a child, if he be capable of salvation, is not capable of receiving. I would have children taught all the great doctrines of truth without a solitary exception, that they may in their after days hold fast by them.

I can bear witness that children *can* understand the Scriptures; for I am sure that, when but a child, I could have discussed many a knotty point of controversial theology, having heard both sides of the question freely stated among my father's circle of friends. In fact, children are capable of understanding some things in early life, which we hardly understand afterwards. Children have eminently a simplicity of faith, and simplicity of faith is akin to the highest knowledge; indeed, we know not that there is much distinction between

the simplicity of a child and the genius of the pro-
foundest mind. He who receives things simply, as
a child, will often have ideas which the man who is
prone to make a syllogism of everything will never
attain unto. If you wish to know whether children
can be taught, I point you to many in our churches,
and in pious families,—not prodigies, but such as
we frequently see,—Timothys and Samuels, and
little girls, too, who have early come to know a
Saviour's love. As soon as a child is capable of
being lost, it is capable of being saved. As soon
as a child can sin, that child can, if God's grace
assist it, believe and receive the Word of God. As
soon as children can learn evil, be assured that they
are competent, under the teaching of the Holy
Spirit, to learn good. Never go to your class with
the thought that the children cannot comprehend
you ; for if you do not make them understand, it
is possibly because you do not yourselves understand ; if you do not teach children what you wish
them to learn, it may be because you are not fit for
the task ; you should find out simpler words, more
fitted for their capacity, and then you would discover
that it was not the fault of the child, but the fault
of the teacher, if he did not learn. I hold that
children are capable of salvation. He who, in
Divine sovereignty, reclaimed the grey-haired
sinner from the error of his ways, can turn a little
child from his youthful follies. He who, in the
eleventh hour, findeth some standing idle in the
market-place, and sendeth them into the vineyard,
can and does call men at the dawning of the day

to labour for Him. He who can change the course of a river when it has rolled onward, and become a mighty flood, can control a new-born rivulet leaping from its cradle-fountain, and make it run into the channel He desireth. He can do all things: He can work upon children's hearts as He pleases, for all are under His control.

I will not stay to establish the doctrine, because I do not consider that any are so foolish as to doubt it. But, although you believe it, I fear many do not expect to hear of children being saved. Throughout the churches, I have noticed a kind of abhorrence of anything like child-piety. We are frightened at the idea of a little boy loving Christ; and if we hear of a little girl following the Saviour, we say it is a youthful fancy, an early impression that will die away. I beseech you, never treat child-piety with suspicion. It is a tender plant; do not brush it too hard. I heard a tale, some time ago, which I believe to be perfectly authentic. A dear little girl, some five or six years old, a true lover of Jesus, requested of her mother that she might join the church. The mother told her she was too young, and the poor little thing was exceedingly grieved. After a while, the mother, who saw that piety was in her child's heart, spoke to the minister on the subject. The minister talked to the child, and said to the mother, " I am thoroughly convinced of her piety, but I cannot take her into the church, she is too young." When the child heard that, a strange gloom passed over her face; and the next morning, when the mother went to

her little bed, she lay with a pearly tear on each
eye, dead for very grief; her heart was broken,
because she could not follow her Saviour, and do
as He had bidden her. I would not have murdered
that child for a world! Take care how you treat
young piety. Be very tender in dealing with it.
Believe that children can be saved just as much as
yourselves. I do most firmly believe in the salvation of children. When you see the young heart
brought to the Saviour, do not stand by and speak
harshly, mistrusting everything. It is better sometimes to be deceived than to be the means of
offending one of these little ones who believe in
Jesus. God send to His people a firm belief that
little buds of grace are worthy of all tender care!

KING DAVID'S TWO ENCOURAGE-
MENTS TO PARENTS AND TEACHERS.

HE first is that of pious example. David said, "Come, ye children, hearken unto me: I will teach you the fear of the Lord." You are not ashamed to tread in the footsteps of David, are you? You will not object to follow the example of one who was first eminently holy, and then eminently great. Shall the shepherd boy, the giant-slayer, the sweet psalmist of Israel, and the mighty monarch, leave footprints in which you are too proud to tread? Ah, no! you will be happy, I am sure, to be as David was. If you want, however, a higher example even than that of David, hear the Son of David while from His lips flow the sweet words, "Suffer the little children to come unto Me, and forbid them not, for of such is the Kingdom of Heaven." I am sure it would encourage you if you always thought of these examples. You who are teaching children, are not dishonoured by that occupation; some may say, "You are only a Sunday-school teacher," but you are a noble personage, holding an honourable office, and having illustrious predecessors. We love to see persons of some standing in society take an interest in Sabbath-schools. One great fault in many of our churches is that the children are left for the young people to care for; the older members, who have more wisdom, taking but very little notice of them; and, very often, the wealthier members of the church stand aside as if the teaching of the poor were not (as indeed it is) the special business of the rich. I hope for the day when the mighty men of Israel shall be found helping in this great warfare against the enemy. In the United States we have heard of Presidents, of Judges, Members of Congress, and persons in the highest positions, not condescending, for I scorn to use such a term, but honouring themselves by teaching little children in Sabbath-schools. He who teaches a class in a Sabbath-school has earned a good degree. I had rather receive the title of S.S.T. than M.A., B.A., or any other honour that ever was conferred by men. Let me beg you, then, to take heart, because your duties are so honourable. Let the royal example of David, let the Godlike example of Jesus Christ inspire you with fresh diligence and increasing ardour, with confident and enduring perseverance, still to go on in your blessed work, saying as David did, "Come, ye children, hearken unto me: I will teach you the fear of the Lord."

The second is the encouragement of great success. David said, " Come, ye children, hearken unto me : " he did not add, " perhaps I will teach you the fear of the Lord," but, " I *will* teach you." He had success ; or, if he had not, others have. The success of Sabbath-schools ! If I begin to talk of that, I shall have an endless theme ; therefore, I will not commence. Many volumes might be written on it, and then when all were written, we might say, " I suppose that even the world itself could not contain all that might be written." Up yonder, where the starry hosts perpetually sing God's high praises, up where the white-robed throng cast their crowns before His feet, we shall behold the success of Sabbath-schools. There, too, where infant millions assemble Sabbath after Sabbath, to sing,—

" Gentle Jesus, meek and mild,"

we see with joy the success of Sabbath-schools. And up here, in almost every pulpit of our land, and there in the pews where the deacons sit, and godly members join in worship, there is seen the success of Sabbath-schools. And far away across yonder broad ocean, in the islets of the South, in lands where those dwell who bow before blocks of wood and stone, there are the missionaries who were saved in Sabbath-schools, and the thousands, blessed by their labours, contribute to swell the mighty stream of the incalculable, I had almost said infinite, success of Sabbath-school instruction. Go on with your holy service; much has been done already, but more shall yet be done.   Let all your past victories inflame you with fresh ardour, let the remembrance of your triumphs in previous campaigns, and all trophies won for your Saviour on the battle-field of the past be your encouragement to press on with the duty of the present and the future.

CHILDHOOD AND HOLY SCRIPTURE.*

PAUL taught young Timothy the gospel himself: he made him not only hear his doctrine, but see his practice. We cannot force truth upon men, but we can make our own teaching clear and decided, and make our lives consistent therewith. Truth and holiness are the surest antidotes to error and unrighteousness. The apostle said to Timothy, "Continue thou in the things which thou hast learned and hast been assured of, knowing of whom thou hast learned them."

He then dwelt upon another potent remedy which had been of great service to the young preacher—namely, the knowing of the Holy Scriptures from his earliest childhood. This was to young Timothy one of his best safeguards. His early training held him like an anchor, and saved him from the dreadful drift of the age. Happy young man, of whom the apostle could say, "From a child thou hast known the Holy Scriptures, which are able

---

* 2 Tim. iii. 15.

to make thee wise unto salvation through faith which is in Christ Jesus"!

To be prepared for the coming conflict, we have only to preach the gospel, and to live the gospel; and also to take care that we teach the children the Word of the Lord. This last is specially to be attended to, for it is by the mouth of babes and sucklings that God will still the enemy. It is idle to dream that human learning must be met by human learning, or that Satan must cast out Satan. No. Lift up the brazen serpent wherever the fiery serpents are biting the people, and men shall look to it and live. Bring the children out, and hold them up, and turn their little eyes towards the divinely ordained remedy; for still there is life in a look—life as against the varied venoms of the serpent which are now poisoning the blood of men. There is no cure after all for midnight but the rising sun; no hope remains for a dark world but in that light which lighteneth every man. Shine forth, O Sun of Righteousness, and mist, and cloud, and darkness must disappear. Keep to the apostolic plans, and rest assured of apostolic success. Preach Christ; preach the Word in season and out of season: and teach the children. One of God's chief methods for preserving His fields from tares, is to sow them early with wheat.

The work of God's grace in Timothy commenced with early instruction—"From a child thou hast known the Holy Scriptures."

Note the time for instruction. The expression,

"from a child," might be better understood if we read it, "from a very child;" or, as the Revised Version has it, "from a babe." It does not mean a well-grown child, or youth, but a child just rising out of infancy. From a very child Timothy had known the sacred writings. This expression is, no doubt, used to show that we cannot begin too early to imbue the minds of our children with Scriptural knowledge. Babes receive impressions long before we are aware of the fact. During the first months of a child's life it learns more than we imagine. It soon learns the love of its mother, and its own dependence; and if the mother be wise, it learns the meaning of obedience and the necessity of yielding its will to a higher will. This may be the key-note of its whole future life. If it learn obedience and submission early, it may save a thousand tears from the child's eyes, and as many from the mother's heart. A special vantage-ground is lost when even babyhood is left uncultured.

The Holy Scriptures may be learned by children as soon as they are capable of understanding anything. It is a very remarkable fact, which I have heard asserted by many teachers, that children will learn to read out of the Bible better than from any other book. I scarcely know why: it may, perhaps, be on account of the simplicity of the language; but I believe it is so. A Biblical fact will often be grasped when an incident of common history is forgotten. There is an adaptation in the Bible for human beings of all ages, and therefore it has a fitness for children. We make a

mistake when we think that we must begin with
something else and lead up to the Scriptures. The
Bible is the book for the peep of day. Parts of it
are above a child's mind, for they are above the
comprehension of the most advanced among us.
There are depths in it wherein leviathan may
swim ; but there are also brooks in which a lamb
may wade. Wise teachers know how to lead
their little ones into the green pastures beside the
still waters.

I was noticing, in the life of that man of God
whose loss presses very heavily upon many of our
hearts—namely, the Earl of Shaftesbury—that his
first religious impressions were produced by a
humble woman. The impressions which made
him—Shaftesbury—the man of God, and the friend
of man, were received in the nursery. Little Lord
Ashley had a godly nurse who spoke to him of the
things of God. He tells us that she died before he
was seven years of age ; clear proof that early in
life his heart had been able to receive the seal of
the Spirit of God, and to receive it by humble
instrumentality. Blessed among women was she
whose name we know not, but who wrought
incalculable service for God and man by her
holy teaching of the chosen child. Young nurses,
note this.

Give us the first seven years of a child, with
God's grace, and we may defy the world, the flesh,
and the devil to ruin that immortal soul. Those
first years, while yet the clay is soft and plastic, go
far to decide the form of the vessel. Do not say

that your office, you who teach the young, is in the least degree inferior to ours, whose main business is with older folks. No, you have the first of them, and your impressions, as they come first, will endure last ; oh, that they may be good, and only good ! Among the thoughts that come to an old man before he enters Heaven, the most plentiful are those that aforetime visited him when he sat upon his mother's knee. That which made Dr. Guthrie ask for a " bairn's hymn " when he was dying, is but an instinct of our nature, which leads us to complete the circle by folding together the ends of life. Childlike things are dearest to old age. We shuffle off a portion of the coil that doth surround and hamper us, and go back again to our more natural selves ; and therefore the old songs are on our lips, and the old thoughts are in our minds. The teachings of our childhood leave clean-cut and sharp impressions upon the mind, which remain after seventy years have passed. Let us see that such impressions are made for the highest ends.

It is well to *note the admirable selection of instructors.* We are not at a loss to tell who instructed youthful Timothy. In the first chapter of this epistle Paul says, " When I call to remembrance the unfeigned faith that is in thee, which dwelt first in thy grandmother Lois, and thy mother Eunice ; and I am persuaded that in thee also." No doubt grandmother Lois and mother Eunice united in teaching the little one. Who should teach the children but the parents ? Timothy's father was a

Greek, and probably a heathen, but his child was happy in having a venerable grandmother, so often the dearest of all relatives to a little child. He had also a gracious mother, once a devout Jewess, and afterwards also a firmly believing Christian, who made it her daily pleasure to teach her own dear child the Word of the Lord. O dear mothers, you have a very sacred trust reposed in you by God! He hath in effect said to you, " Take this child and nurse it for Me, and I will give thee thy wages." You are called to equip the future man of God, that he may be thoroughly furnished unto every good work. If God spares you, you may live to hear that pretty boy speak to thousands, and you will have the sweet reflection in your heart that the quiet teachings of the nursery led the man to love his God and serve Him. Those who think that a woman detained at home by her little family is doing nothing, think the reverse of what is true. Scarcely can the godly mother quit her home for a place of worship ; but dream not that she is lost to the work of the church ; far from it, she is doing the best possible service for her Lord. Mothers, the godly training of your offspring is your first and most pressing duty. Christian women, by teaching children the Holy Scriptures, are as much fulfilling their part for the Lord, as Moses in judging Israel, or Solomon in building the temple.

WITNESSES FOR GOD CONVERTED IN YOUTH.*

 SUSPECT that Elijah did not think very much of Obadiah. He does not treat him with any great consideration, but addresses him more sharply than one would expect from a fellow-believer. Elijah was the man of action — bold, always to the front, with nothing to conceal; Obadiah was a quiet believer, true and steadfast, but in a very difficult position, and therefore driven to perform his duty in a less open manner. His faith in the Lord swayed his life, but did not drive him out of the court. I notice that even after Elijah had learned more of him at this interview, he speaks concerning God's people as if he did not reckon much upon Obadiah, and others like him. He says, "They have thrown down Thine altars, and slain Thy prophets with the sword; and I, even I only, am left; and they seek my life, to take it away." He knew very well that Obadiah was left, who, though not exactly a

---

prophet, was a man of mark ; but he seems to ignore him as if he were of small account in the great struggle. I suppose it was because this man of iron, this prophet of fire and thunder, this mighty servant of the Most High, set small store by anybody who did not come to the front and fight like himself. I know it is the tendency of brave and zealous minds somewhat to undervalue quiet, retired piety. True and accepted servants of God may be doing their best under great disadvantages, against fierce opposition, but they may scarcely be known, and may even shun the least recognition ; therefore men who live in the fierce light of public life are apt to under-estimate them. These minor stars are lost in the brilliance of the man whom God lights up like a new sun to flame through the darkness. Elijah flashed over the sky of Israel like a thunderbolt from the hand of the Eternal, and naturally he would be somewhat impatient of those whose movements were slower and less conspicuous. It is Martha and Mary over again, in some respects.

The Lord does not love that His servants, however great they are, should think lightly of their lesser comrades, and it occurs to me that He so arranged matters that Obadiah became important to Elijah when he had to face the wrathful king of Israel. The prophet is bidden to go and show himself to Ahab, and he does so ; but he judges it better to begin by showing himself to the governor of his palace, that he may break the news to his master, and prepare him for the interview. Ahab was exasperated by the terrible results of the long drought, and might in his sudden fury attempt to kill the prophet ; and so he is to have time for consideration, that he may cool down a little.

Elijah has an interview with Obadiah, and bids him go and say to Ahab, "Behold Elijah." It may sometimes be the nearest way to our object to go a little round about. But it is remarkable that Obadiah should thus be made useful to a man so much his superior. He who never feared the face of kings nevertheless found himself using as his helper a far more timid individual.

We learn further from the narrative, that God will never leave Himself without witnesses in this world. Aye, and He will not leave Himself without witnesses in the worst places of the world. What a horrible abode for a true believer Ahab's court must have been ! If there had been no sinner there but that woman Jezebel, she was enough to make the place a sink of iniquity. That strong-minded, proud, Sidonian Queen twisted poor Ahab round her fingers just as she pleased. He might never have been the persecutor he was if his wife had not stirred him up ; but she hated the worship of Jehovah intensely, and despised the homeliness of Israel in comparison with the more pompous style of Sidon. Ahab must yield to her imperious demands, for she would brook no contradiction, and when her proud spirit was roused she defied all opposition. Yet in that very court where Jezebel was mistress, the chamberlain was a man who feared God greatly. Never be surprised to meet with a believer anywhere. Grace can live where you would never expect to see it survive for an hour.

Joseph feared God in the court of Pharaoh, Daniel was a trusted counsellor of Nebuchadnezzar, Mordecai waited at the gate of Ahasuerus, Pilate's wife pleaded for the life of Jesus, and there were saints in Cæsar's household. Think of finding diamonds of the first water on such a dunghill as Nero's palace. Those who feared God in Rome were not only Christians, but they were ensamples to all other Christians for their brotherly love and generosity. Surely there is no place in this land where there is not some light : the darkest cavern of iniquity has its torch. Be not afraid ; you may find followers of Jesus in the precincts of Pandemonium. In the palace of Ahab you meet an Obadiah who rejoices to hold fellowship with despised saints, and quits the levees of a monarch for the hiding places of persecuted ministers.

I notice that these witnesses for God are very often persons converted in their youth. He seems to take a delight to make these His special standard-bearers in the day of battle. Look at Samuel! When all Israel became disgusted with the wickedness of Eli's sons the child Samuel ministered before the Lord. Look at David ! When he is but a shepherd boy he wakes the echoes of the lone hills with his psalms and the accompanying music of his harp. See Josiah ! When Israel had revolted it was a child, Josiah by name, that broke down the altars of Baal and burned the bones of his priests. Daniel was but a youth when he took his stand for purity and God. The Lord hath to-day—I know not where —some little Luther on his mother's knee, some young Calvin learning in our Sunday-school, some youthful Zwingle singing a hymn to Jesus. This age may grow worse and worse ; I sometimes think it will, for many signs look that way ; but the Lord is preparing for it. The days are dark and ominous ; and this eventide may darken down into a blacker night than has been known before ; but God's cause is safe in God's hands. His work will not tarry for want of men. Put not forth the hand of Uzzah to steady the ark of the Lord ; it shall go safely on in God's predestined way. Christ will not fail nor be discouraged. God buries His workmen, but His work lives on. If there be not in the palace a king who honours God there shall yet be found there a governor who fears the Lord from his youth, who shall take care of the Lord's prophets, and hide them away till better days shall come. Wherefore be of good courage, and look for happier hours. Nothing of real value is in jeopardy while Jehovah is on the throne. The Lord's reserves are coming up, and their drums beat victory.

OBADIAH'S EARLY PIETY.

BADIAH possessed *early piety*—" I thy
servant fear the Lord from my youth."
Oh, that all our youth who may grow up
to manhood and womanhood may be able
to say the same! Happy are the people
who are in such a case!

How Obadiah came to fear the Lord in youth we
cannot tell. The instructor by whom he was led
to faith in Jehovah is not mentioned. Yet we may
reasonably conclude that he had believing parents.
Slender as the ground may seem to be, I think it
is pretty firm, when I remind you of *his name*.
This would very naturally be given him by his father
or his mother, and as it signifies "the servant of
Jehovah," I should think it indicated his parents' piety.
In the days when there was persecution everywhere
against the faithful, and the name of Jehovah was
in contempt because the calves of Bethel and the
images of Baal were set up everywhere, I do not
think that unbelieving parents would have given to
their child the name of " The servant of Jehovah,"
if they themselves had not felt a reverence for the

Lord. They would not idly have courted the re-
marks of their idolatrous neighbours, and the enmity
of the great. In a time when names meant something, they would have called him "The child of
Baal," or "The servant of Chemosh," or some other
name expressive of reverence to the popular gods,
if the fear of God had not been before their eyes.
The selection of such a name betrays to me their
earnest desire that their boy might grow up to serve
Jehovah, and never bow his knee before the abhorred
idols of the Sidonian queen. Whether this be so or
not, it is quite certain that thousands of the most
intelligent believers owe their first bent towards
godliness to the sweet associations of home. How
many of us might well have borne some such a
name as that of Obadiah ; for no sooner did we see
the light than our parents tried to enlighten us with
the truth. We were consecrated to the service of
God before we knew that there was a God. Many
a tear of earnest prayer fell on our infant brow and
sealed us for Heaven ; we were nursed in the atmos-
phere of devotion ; there was scarce a day in which
we were not urged to be faithful servants of God,
and entreated while we were yet young to seek
Jesus and give our hearts to Him.

If he had no gracious parents, I cannot tell how
Obadiah came to be a believer in the Lord in those
sad days, unless he fell in with some kind teacher,
tender nurse, or perhaps good servant in his father's
house, or pious neighbour, who dared to gather
little children round about him and tell of the Lord
God of Israel. Some holy woman may have in-

stilled the law of the Lord into his young mind
before the priests of Baal could poison him with
their falsehoods. No mention is made of anybody
in connection with this man's conversion in his
youth, and it does not matter, does it? You and
I do not want to be mentioned if we are right-
hearted servants of God.

This early piety of Obadiah's had special marks
of genuineness about it. The way in which he
described it is very instructive, "I thy servant fear
the Lord from my youth." I hardly remember in
all my life to have heard the piety of children
described in ordinary conversation by this term,
though it is the common word of the Scriptures.
We say, "The dear child loved God." We talk of
their "being made so happy," and so forth, and I
do not question the rightness of the language;
still, the Holy Spirit speaks of "the fear of the
Lord" as "the beginning of wisdom;" and David
says, "Come, ye children, hearken unto me: I will
teach you the fear of the Lord." Children will
get great joy through faith in the Lord Jesus; but
that joy, if true, is full of lowly reverence and awe
of the Lord.

You do not need that I should speak to you at
large upon the advantages of early piety. I will,
therefore, only sum them up in a few sentences. To
be a believer in God early in life is to be saved from
a thousand regrets. Such a man shall never have
to say that he carries in his bones the sins of his
youth. Early piety helps us to form associations
for the rest of life which will prove helpful, and it

saves us from those which are harmful. The Christian young man will not fall into the common sins of young men, and injure his constitution by excesses. He will be likely to be married to a Christian woman, and so to have a holy companion in his march towards Heaven. He will select as his associates those who will be his friends in the church and not in the tavern ; his helpers in virtue, and not his tempters to vice. Depend upon it, a great deal depends upon whom we choose for our companions when we begin life. If we start in bad company, it is very hard to break away from it. The man brought to Christ early in life has this further advantage, that he is helped to form holy habits and he is saved from being the slave of their opposites. Habits soon become a second nature ; to form new ones is hard work ; but those formed in youth remain in old age. There is something in that verse,—

> "'Tis easier work if we begin
>   To serve the Lord betimes ;
> But sinners who grow old in sin
>   Are hardened in their crimes."

I am sure it is so. Moreover, I notice that, very frequently, those who are brought to Christ whilst young grow in grace more rapidly and readily than others do. They have not so much to unlearn, and they have not such a heavy weight of old memories to carry. The scars and bleeding sores which come of having spent years in the service of the devil are missed by those whom the Lord brings into His church before they have wandered far into the world.

As to early piety in its bearing upon others, I cannot too highly commend it. How attractive it is! Grace looks loveliest in youth. That which would not be noticed in the grown-up man, strikes at once the most careless observer when seen in a child. Grace in a child has a convincing force: the infidel drops his weapon and admires. A word spoken by a child abides in the memory, and its artless accents touch the heart. Where the minister's sermon fails, the child's prayer may gain the victory. Moreover, religion in children suggests encouragement to those of riper years; for others seeing the little one saved say to themselves, " Why should not we also find the Lord?" By a certain secret power it opens closed doors, and turns the key in the lock of unbelief. Where nothing else could win a way for truth, a child's love has done it. It is still true, " Out of the mouth of babes and sucklings hast Thou ordained strength because of Thine enemies, that Thou mightest still the enemy and the avenger."

OBADIAH AND ELIJAH.

YOUTHFUL piety leads on to persevering piety. Obadiah could say, "I thy servant fear the Lord from my youth." Time had not changed him : whatever his age may have been, his religion had not decayed. We are all fond of novelty, and I have known some men go wrong, as it were, for a change. It is not burning quick to the death in martyrdom that is the hard work ; roasting before a slow fire is a far more terrible test of firmness. To continue gracious during a long life of temptation is to be gracious indeed. For the grace of God to convert a man like Paul, who is full of threatenings against the saints, is a great marvel ; but for the grace of God to preserve a believer for ten, twenty, thirty, forty, fifty years, is quite as great a miracle and deserves more of our praise than it usually commands. Obadiah was not affected by the lapse of time ; he was found to be when old what he was when young.

Nor was he carried away by the fashion of those evil times. To be a servant of Jehovah was thought to be a mean thing, old-fashioned, ignorant, a thing of the past; the worship of Baal was the " modern thought " of the hour. All the court walked after the god of Sidon, and all the courtiers went in the same way. My lord worshipped Baal, and my lady worshipped Baal, for the Queen worshipped Baal; but Obadiah said, " I thy servant fear Jehovah from my youth." Blessed is the man who cares nothing for the fashion, for it passeth away. If for a while it rageth towards evil, what hath the believing man to do but to abide steadfastly by the right? Obadiah was not even affected by the absence of the means of grace. The priests and Levites had fled into Judah, and the prophets had been killed or hidden away, and there was no public worship of Jehovah in Israel. The temple was far away at Jerusalem; therefore he had no opportunity of hearing anything that could strengthen him or stimulate him; yet he held on his way.

Added to this, there were the difficulties of his position. He was chamberlain of the palace. If he had pleased Jezebel and worshipped Baal he might have been much easier in his situation, for he would have enjoyed her royal patronage; but there he was, governor in Ahab's house, and yet fearing Jehovah. He must have had to walk very delicately, and watch his words most carefully. I do not wonder that he became a very cautious person, and was a little afraid even of Elijah, lest he was giving him a commission which would lead to his destruction. He came to be extremely prudent, and looked on things round about so as neither to compromise his conscience nor jeopardise his position. It wants an uncommonly wise man to do that, but he who can accomplish it is to be commended. He did not run away from his position, nor retreat from his religion. If he had been forced to do wrong, I am sure he would have imitated the priests and Levites and have fled into Judah, where the worship of Jehovah continued ; but he felt that without yielding to idolatry he could do something for God in his advantageous position, and therefore he determined to stop and fight it out. When there is no hope of victory you may as well retire ; but he is the brave man who when the bugle sounds retreat does not hear it, who puts his blind eye to the telescope and cannot see the signal to cease firing, but just holds his position against all odds, and does all the damage he can to the enemy. Obadiah was a man who did in truth " hold the fort," for he felt that when all the prophets were doomed by Jezebel it was his part to stay near the tigress and save the lives of at least a hundred servants of God from her cruel power. If he could not do more he would not have lived in vain if he accomplished so much. I admire the man whose decision was equal to his prudence, though I should greatly fear to occupy so perilous a place. His course was something like walking on the tight rope with Blondin. I should not like to try it myself, nor would I recommend any of you to attempt a feat so difficult. The part of Elijah is much safer and grander. The

prophet's course was plain enough ; he had not to
please, but to reprove Ahab ; he had not to be
wary, but to act in a bold outspoken manner for
the God of Israel.   How much the greater man he
seems to be when the two stand together in the
scene before us.   Obidiah falls on his face and calls
him " My lord Elijah ; " and well he might, for
he was far his inferior.   Yet I must not fall morally
into Elijah's vein myself, lest I have to pull myself
up with a sharp check.   It was a great thing for
Obadiah that he could manage Ahab's household
with Jezebel in it, and yet, for all that, win this
commendation from the Spirit of God, that _he
feared the Lord greatly_.

He persevered, too, notwithstanding his success
in life ; and that I hold to be much to his credit.
There is nothing more perilous to a man than to
prosper in this world and become rich and respect-
able.   Of course we desire it, wish for it, strive for
it ; but how many in winning it have lost all, as
to spiritual wealth !   The man used to love the
people of God, and now he says, "They are a
vulgar class of persons."   So long as he could hear
the gospel he did not mind the architecture of the
house ; but now he has grown æsthetic, and must
have a spire, Gothic architecture, a marble pulpit,
priestly millinery, a conservatory in the church,
and all sorts of pretty things.   As he has filled his
pocket he has emptied his brains, and especially
emptied his heart.   He has got away from truth and
principle in proportion as he has made an advance
in his estate.   This is a mean business, which at

one time he would have been the first to condemn. There is no chivalry in such conduct ; it is dastardly to the last degree. God save us from it ; but a great many people are not saved from it. Their religion is not a matter of principle, but a matter of interest : it is not the pursuit of truth, but a hankering after society, whatever that may mean ; it is not their object to glorify God, but to get rich husbands for their girls ; it is not conscience that guides them, but the hope of being able to invite Sir John to dinner with them, and of dining at the Hall in return. Do not think I am sarcastic : I speak in sober sadness of things which make one feel ashamed. I hear of them daily, though they do not personally affect me. This is an age of meannesses disguised under the notion of respectability. God send us men of the stuff of John Knox, or, if you prefer it, of the adamantine metal of Elijah ; and if these should prove too stiff and stern we could even be content with such men as Obadiah. Possibly these last might be harder to produce than Elijahs : but with God all things are possible.

Obadiah, with his early grace and persevering decision, became a man of eminent piety, and this is the more remarkable considering what he was and where he was. Eminent piety in a Lord High Chamberlain of Ahab's court ! This is a wonder of grace indeed. This man's religion was intense within him. If he did not make the open use of it that Elias did, he was not called to such a career but it dwelt deep within his soul, and others knew it. Jezebel knew it, I have no doubt whatever. She did not like him, but she had to endure him ; she looked askance at him, but she could not dislodge him. Ahab had learned to trust him and could not do without him, for he probably furnished him with a little strength of mind. Possibly Ahab liked to retain him just to show Jezebel that he could be obstinate if he liked, and was still a man.

Account for it how you may, it is singular that in the centre of rebellion against God there was one whose devotion to God was intense. As it is horrible to find a Judas among the apostles, so it is grand to discover an Obadiah among Ahab's courtiers. What grace must have been at work to maintain such a fire in the midst of the sea, such godliness in the midst of the vilest iniquity !

Obadiah's early religion became comfortable piety to him afterwards. When he thought Elijah was about to expose him to great danger he pleaded his long service of God, saying, "I thy servant fear the Lord from my youth" ; just as David, when he grew old, said, " O God, Thou hast taught me from my youth : and hitherto have I declared Thy wondrous works ; now also when I am old and greyheaded, O God, forsake me not." It will be a great comfort to people, when old, to look back upon a life spent in the service of God. You will not trust in it, you will not think that there is any merit in it ; but you will bless God for it. A servant who has been with his master from his youth ought not to be turned adrift when he grows

grey.   A right-minded master respects the person
who has served him long and well.   Suppose you
had living in the family an old nurse who had
nursed you when you were a child, and had lived
to bring up your children, would you turn her into
the street when she was past her work?   No ; you
will do your best for her ; if it is in your power
you will keep her out of the workhouse.   Now, the
Lord is much more kind and gracious than we are,
and He will never turn off His old servants.

ABIJAH'S "SOME GOOD THING."*

JEROBOAM had proved false to the Lord who had placed him upon the throne of Israel, and the time was come for his overthrow. The Lord, who usually brings forth the rod before He lifts the axe, sent sickness into his house: his son Abijah was sore sick. Then the parents bethought them of an old prophet of God, and desired to know through him what would happen to the child. Fearful lest the prophet should denounce plagues upon him and his child if he knew that the enquirer was the wife of Jeroboam, the king begged the Egyptian princess whom he had married to disguise herself as a farmer's wife, and so get from the man of God a more favourable answer. Poor foolish king, to imagine that a prophet who could see into futurity could not also see through any disguise with which his queen might surround herself! So anxious was the mother to know the fate of her son, that

* 1 Kings xiv. 13.

she left his sick-chamber to go to Shiloh to hear
the sentence of the prophet.   Vain was her clever
disguise! the blind prophet was still a seer, and not
only discerned her before she entered the house,
but saw the future of her family.   She came full
of superstition to be told her fortune, but she went
away heavy, having been told her faults and her
doom.

In the terrible tidings which the prophet Ahijah
delivered to this wife of Jeroboam, there was only
one bright spot, only one word of solace; and I
am greatly afraid that it gave no kind of comfort
to the heathen queen.   The child was mercifully
appointed to die, for in him there was " found some
good thing toward Jehovah, God of Israel."

We are going to look into the little that we know
of the young prince Abijah.   His name was a
suitable one.   A good name may belong to a very
bad man ; but in this case a gracious name was
worthily worn.   He called God his Father, and his
name signifies that fact.   *Ab*, you know, is the word
for *Father*, and *Jah* is *Jehovah*—Jehovah was his
Father.   I would not have mentioned the name had
not his life made it true.   Oh, you who bear good
Bible names, see that you do not dishonour them !

There was in this child " some good thing toward
the Lord God of Israel ;" but what was it ?   Who
shall define it ?   A boundless field for conjecture
opens before us.   We know there was in him *some*
good thing, but what form that good thing took we
do not know.   Tradition has made assertions, but
as these are mere inventions to fill up a gap, they

are scarcely worth mentioning. Our own reflections
will, probably, be as near the mark as these im-
probable traditions. We may learn much from the
silence of Scripture : we are not told precisely what
the good thing was, because any good thing towards
the Lord is a sufficient sign of grace. Though
the child's *faith* is not mentioned, we are sure that
he had faith in the living God, since without it
nothing in him would have been good towards God ;
for "without faith it is impossible to please God."
He was a child believer in Jehovah, the God of
Israel : perhaps his mother left him at his own
request to go to the Lord's prophet about him.
Many false prophets were around the palace : his
father might not have sent to Shiloh, had not the
boy pleaded for it. The child believed in the great
invisible God, who made the heavens and the earth,
and he worshipped Him in faith. I should not
wonder, however, if in that child his *love* was more
apparent than his faith ; for converted children
more usually talk of loving Christ than they do of
trusting in Him : not because faith is not in them,
but because the emotion of love is more congenial
to the child's nature than the more intellectual act
of faith. The heart is large in the child, and therefore love becomes his most conspicuous fruit. I
have no doubt this child showed an early affection
towards the unseen Jehovah, and a distaste for the
idols of his father's court. Possibly he displayed
a holy horror of the worship of God under the
figure of a calf. Even a child would have intelli-
gence enough to perceive that it must be wrong to

liken the great and glorious God to a bullock which
hath horns and hoofs.   Perhaps the child's refined
nature also started back from those base priests of
the lowest of the land whom his father had raked
together.   We do not know exactly the form it
took, but there it was : "some good thing" was in
the child's heart towards Jehovah, God of Israel.

It was not merely a good inclination which was
in him, nor a good desire, but a really good, sub-
stantial virtue.   There was in him a true and sub-
stantial existence of grace, and this is far more
than a transient desire.   What child is there that
has not at some time or other, if it has been trained
in the fear of God, felt tremblings of heart and
desires towards God ?   Such goodness is as common as the early dew ; but alas ! it passeth away
quite as speedily.   The young Abijah possessed
something within him sufficiently real and sub-
stantial to be called a " good *thing*" ; the Spirit of
God had wrought a sure work upon him, and left
within him a priceless jewel of grace.   Let us
admire this good thing, though we cannot precisely
describe it.

Let us admire, also, that this "some good thing"
should have been in the child's heart, for *its entrance
is unknown*.   We cannot tell how grace entered
the palace of Tirzah and gained this youthful heart.
God saw the good thing, for He sees the least good
thing in any of us, since He has a quick eye to
perceive anything that looks toward Himself.   But
how did this gracious work come to the child ?   We
are not told, and this silence is a lesson to us.   It

is not essential to us to know *how* a child receives
grace. We need not be painfully anxious to know
when, or where, or how a child is converted ; it may
even be impossible to tell, for the work may have
been so gradual that day and hour cannot be
known. Even those who are converted in riper
years cannot all describe their conversion in detail,
much less can we expect to map out the experience of children who have never gone into outward sin, but under the restraints of godly education
have kept the commandments from their youth up,
like the young man in the gospel narrative. How
came this child to have this good thing in his heart ?
So far we know : we are sure that God placed it
there ; but by what means ? The child, in all
probability, did not hear the teaching of the prophets
of God ; he was never, like young Samuel, taken
up to the house of the Lord. His mother was an
idolatrous princess, his father was among the most
wicked of men, and yet the grace of God reached
their child. Did the Spirit of the Lord operate
upon his heart through his own thoughts ? Did he
think over the matter, and did he come to the con-
clusion that God was God, and that He must not
be worshipped as his father worshipped Him, under
the image of a calf? Even a child might see this.
Had some hymn to Jehovah been sung under the
palace wall by some lone worshipper ? Had the
child seen his father on that day when he lifted up
his hand against the prophet of Jehovah at the
altar of Bethel, when suddenly his right hand
withered at his side ? Did the tears start from the

boy's eye when he saw his father thus paralyzed in
the arm of his strength? and did he laugh for very
joy of heart when by the prophet's prayer his
father was restored again?   Did that great miracle
of mercy cause him to love the God of Israel?   Is
it a mere fancy that this may have been so?   A
withered right hand in a father, and that father a
king, is a thing a child is pretty sure to be told of,
and if it be restored by prayer the wonder would
naturally fill the palace, and be spoken of by everybody, and the prince would hear of it.   Or what if
this little child had a godly nurse?   What if some
girl like her that waited upon Naaman's wife was
the messenger of love to him?   As she carried him
to and fro, did his nurse sing him one of the songs
of Zion, and tell him of Joseph and Samuel?
Israel had not yet so long forsaken her God as to
be without many a faithful follower of the God of
Abraham, and perhaps by one of these sufficient
knowledge was conveyed to the child to become
the means of conveying the love of God to his
soul. We may conjecture, but we may not pretend
to be sure that it was so, nor is there any need that
we should be. If the sun be risen it matters little
when the day first dawned. Be it ours when we see
in children some good thing to rest content with
that truth, even if we cannot tell how it came there.
God's electing love is never short of means to carry
out its purpose : He can send His effectual grace
into the heart of Jeroboam's family, and while the
father is prostrate before his idols the Lord can find
a true worshipper for Himself in the king's own

child. " Out of the mouths of babes and sucklings
hast Thou ordained strength because of Thine
enemies." Thy footsteps are not always seen, O
God of grace, but we have learned to adore Thee
in Thy work, even when we discern not Thy way.

This " good thing " is described in a certain
measure. It was a " good thing toward Jehovah,
the God of Israel." The good thing looked towards the living God. In children there often will
be found good things towards their parents : let
these be cultivated—but these are not sufficient
evidences of grace. In children there will sometimes be found good things towards amiability and
moral excellence : let all good things be commended
and fostered, but they are not sure fruits of grace.
It is towards God that the good thing must be that
saves the soul. Remember how we read in the New
Testament of repentance towards God and of faith
in our Lord Jesus Christ. The way the face of the
good thing looks is a main point about it. There
is life in a look. If a man be travelling away from
God, every step he takes increases his distance from
Him ; but if his face be toward the Lord, he may
be only capable of a child's tottering step, but yet
he is moving nearer and nearer every moment.
There was some good thing in this child *towards
God*, and that is the most distinguishing mark of a
truly good thing. The child had love, and there
was in it love to Jehovah. He had faith, but it was
faith in Jehovah. His religious fear was the fear
of the living God ; his childlike thoughts, and
desires, and prayers, and hymns, went towards the

true God. This is what we desire to see not only in children, but in adults ; we wish to see their hearts turned to the Lord, and their minds and wills moving towards the Most High.

In this dear child, that "good thing" wrought such an outward character that he became exceedingly well beloved. We are sure of that, because it is said "all Israel shall mourn for him." He was probably the heir to his father's crown, and there were godly but grieved hearts in Israel that hoped to see times of reform when that youth should come to the throne ; and perhaps even those who did not care about religion, yet somehow had marked the youth, and observed his going in and out before them, and had said, "He is Israel's hope ; there will be better days when that boy becomes a man ; " so that when Abijah died, he alone of all his race received both tears and a tomb ; he died lamented, and was buried with respect, whereas all the rest of Jeroboam's house were devoured of dogs and vultures. It is a very blessed thing when there is such a good thing in our children that they come to be beloved in their little spheres. They have not all the range which this young prince enjoyed so as to secure universal admiration ; but still the grace of God in a child is a very lovely thing, and it draws forth general approbation. Youthful piety is a very touching thing to me ; I see the grace of God in men and women with much thankfulness, but I cannot perceive it in children without shedding tears of delight. There is an exceeding beauty about these rosebuds of the Lord's garden ; they have a fragrance which we find not in the fairest of earth's lilies. Love is won for the Lord Jesus in many a heart by these tiny arrows of the Lord, whose very smallness is a part of their power to penetrate the heart. The ungodly may not love the grace which is in the children, but since they love the children in whom that grace is found, they are no longer able to speak against religion as they otherwise would have done. Yea, more, the Holy Spirit uses these children for yet higher ends, and those who see them are often impressed with desires for better things.

ABIJAH'S "SOME GOOD THING."—II.

E did not wear the broad phylactery, but he had a meek and quiet spirit. He may not have been much of a speaker, else it might have been said "He has spoken good things concerning the God of Israel;" he may have been a timid, retiring, almost silent boy, but the good thing was "*in* him." And this is the kind of thing which we desire for every one of our friends, a work of grace *within*. The grand point is not to wear the garb, nor use the brogue of religion, but to possess the life of God *within*, and feel and think as Jesus would have done because of that inner life. Small is the value of external religion unless it be the outcome of a life within. True grace is not as a garment, to be put on and taken off; but it is an integral part of the person who possesses it. This child's piety was of the true, personal, inward kind: may all our children have some good thing *in* them!

We are told that this good thing "was found" in him: this means that it was discernible in him without much difficulty, for the expression " found " is used even when it does not imply any great search. Does not the Lord say, " I am found of them that sought Me not " ? Zealous, child-like piety soon shows itself ; a child is usually far less reticent than a man ; the little lip is not frozen by cold prudence, but reveals the heart. Godliness in a child appears even upon the surface, so that persons who come into the house as visitors are surprised by the artless statements which betray the young Christian. There were many in Tirzah who could not help knowing that this child had in him some good thing towards Jehovah. They may not have cared to see it, they may have hoped that it would be crushed out of him by the example of the court around him, but still they knew that there it was, they had found it without difficulty.

Still, the expression does bear another shade of meaning : it implies that when God, the strict heart-searcher, who trieth the reins of the children of men, visited this child, He found in him some- what unto praise and glory : "some good thing" was discovered in him by those eyes which cannot be deceived. It is not all gold that glitters, but that which was in this child was genuine metal. Oh, that the like may be true of each of us when we are tried as by fire ! It may be that his father was angry with him for serving Jehovah ; but whatever his trial may have been, he came out of it unharmed.

The expression suggests to me somewhat of the idea of surprise. How did this good thing get into

the child? " In him there is *found* some good
thing,"—as when a man findeth a treasure in a
field. The farmer was thinking of nothing but his
oxen, and his acres, and his harvest, when on a
sudden his plough laid bare a hidden treasure : he
found it where it was, but how it came to be there
he could not tell. So in this child, so disadvanta-
geously placed, to the surprise of everybody there
was found some good thing toward the Lord God
of Israel. His conversion, you see, is veiled in
mystery. We are not told of the grace in his
heart what it was, nor whence it came, nor what
special actions it produced, but there it was, *found*
where none expected it. I believe that this case is
typical of many of the elect children whom God
calls by His grace in the courts and alleys of
London. You must not expect that you shall jot
down their experience, and their feelings, and their
lives, and total them all up ; you must not reckon
to know dates and means specifically, but you must
take the child as we have to take Abijah, rejoicing
to find in him a little wonder of grace with God's
own seal upon him. The old prophet, in the name
of the Lord, attested the young prince as a true-
hearted follower of the Most High ; and in like
manner the Lord sets His attesting mark of grace
on regenerated children, and we must be content to
see it, even if some other things be wanting. Let
us welcome with delight those works of the Holy
Spirit which we cannot precisely describe.

All that is said of this case was that there was
in him " some good thing " ; and this reads as if

the Divine work was as yet only a spark of grace,
the beginning of spiritual life.   There was nothing
very striking in him, or it would be more definitely
mentioned.   He was not an heroic follower of
Jehovah, and his deeds of loyalty to God are not
written, because by reason of his tender years he
had neither power nor opportunity to do much
which could be written.   Inasmuch as we read
that in him was "some good thing", it is implied
that it was not a perfect thing, and that it was not
attended with all the good things one might wish
for.   Many good things were missing, but "some
good thing" was manifest, and therefore the child
was accepted, and by Divine love rescued from an
ignoble death.

We are apt to overlook "some good thing" in a
bad house.   This was the most wonderful thing of
all, that there should be a gracious child in
Jeroboam's palace.   The mother usually sways the
house, but the queen was a princess of Egypt and
an idolater.   A father has great influence, but in
this case Jeroboam sinned and made Israel to sin.
It strikes me as a wonder that he should make
Israel to sin, but could not make his child to sin.
All the land feels the pestilent influence of
Jeroboam, and yet close at his feet there is a bright
spot which sovereign grace has kept from the
plague ; his firstborn child, who naturally would
imitate his father, is the very reverse of him—there
is found in Jeroboam's heir "some good thing
toward Jehovah, God of Israel."   In such a place
we do not look for grace, and are apt to pass it by.

If you go to the courts of our great cities, which
are anything but palatial, you will see that they
swarm with the children of the poor, and you
hardly expect to see grace where sin evidently
abounds. In the fever-dens and pestilent alleys of
the great city you hear blasphemy and see
drunkenness on all sides, but do not therefore conclude that no child of God is there ; do not say
within yourself, " The electing love of God has
never pitched upon any of these." How do you
know ? One of those poor little ragged children
playing on a dustheap may have found Christ in
the Ragged-school, and may be destined to a place
at Christ's right hand. Precious is that gem, though
cast amidst these pebbles. Bright is that diamond,
though it lie upon a dunghill. If in the child there
is " some good thing toward the Lord God of
Israel," he is none the less to be valued because his
father is a thief and his mother is a gin-drinker.
Never despise the most ragged child. A clergy-
man in Ireland, ministering to a little Protestant
congregation, noticed for several Sundays, standing
in the aisle near the door, a very ragged boy, who
listened to the sermon most eagerly. He wished
to know who the boy could be, but he always
vanished as soon as the sermon was over. He
asked a friend or two to watch, but somehow the
boy always escaped, and could not be discovered.
It came to pass one Sunday that the minister
preached a sermon from this text, " His own right
hand and His holy arm hath gotten Him the
victory," and after that time he missed the boy

altogether. Six weeks elapsed, and the child did not come any more, but a man appeared from the hills, and begged the minister to come and see his boy, who was dying. He lived in a miserable hovel up in the mountains. A six-mile walk in the rain, through bogs and over hills, and the minister came to the door of the hut. As he entered, the poor lad was sitting up in bed, and as soon as he caught sight of the preacher he waved his arm and cried out, "His own right hand and His holy arm hath gotten Him the victory." That was his closing speech on earth, his dying shout of triumph. Who knows but in many and many a case the Lord's right hand and holy arm have gotten Him the victory, despite the poverty and the sin and the ignorance that may have surrounded the young convert ? Let us not therefore despise grace, wherever it is, but heartily prize what we are apt to overlook.

We cannot understand *that God's dear little children who love Him should often be called to suffer*. We say, "Well, if it was my child I should heal him and ease his sufferings at once." Yet the Almighty Father allows His dear ones to be afflicted. The godly child of Jeroboam lies sick, and yet his wicked father is not sick, and his mother is not sick ; we could almost wish they were, that they might do the less evil. Only one godly one is in the family, and he lies sick ! Why was it so ? Why is it so in other cases ? You shall see a gracious child a cripple, you shall see a heavenly-minded girl a consumptive : you shall often see the heavy hand of God resting where His eternal love has fixed its choice. There is a meaning in all this, and we know somewhat of it ; and if we knew nothing we would believe all the same in the goodness of the Lord. Jeroboam's son was like the fig of the sycamore tree, which does not ripen till it is bruised : by his sickness he was speedily ripened for glory. Besides, it was for his father's good and mother's good that he was sick ; if they had been willing to learn from the sorrow, it might have greatly blessed them. It did drive them to the prophet of God. Oh, that it had driven them to God Himself ! A sick child has led many a blinded parent to the Saviour, and eyes have thereby been opened.

There is something more remarkable still, and that is *that some of God's dearest children should die while they are yet young*. I should have said let Jeroboam die and his wife too, but spare the child. Ay, but the child must go : he is the fittest. His departure was intended to give glory to God's grace in saving such a child, and making him so soon perfect. It was to be the reward of grace, for the child was taken from the evil to come ; he was to die in peace and be buried, whereas the rest of the family would be slain with the sword and given to the jackals and the vultures to tear in pieces. In this child's case his early death was a proof of grace. If any say that converted children ought not to be taken into the church, I answer, How is it the Lord takes so many of them into heaven ? If they are fit for the one, they surely are fit for the other ?

10

The Lord, in infinite mercy, often takes children home to Himself, and saves them from the trials of long life and temptation ; because not only is there grace in them, but there is so much more grace than usual that there is no need for delay, they are ripe already for the harvest. It is wonderful what great grace may dwell in a boy's heart : child piety is by no means of an inferior kind, it is sometimes ripe for heaven.

THE SHUNAMMITE WOMAN'S SON.

LET me call your attention to a most instructive miracle wrought by the prophet Elisha, as recorded in the Book of Kings. The hospitality of the Shunammite woman had been rewarded by the gift of a son; but, alas! all earthly mercies are of uncertain tenure, and after certain days the child fell sick and died.

The distressed but believing mother hastened at once to the man of God; through him God had spoken the promise which fulfilled her heart's desire, and she resolved to plead her case with him, that he might lay it before his Divine Master, and obtain for her an answer of peace. Elisha's action is recorded in the following verses:—

"Then he said to Gehazi, Gird up thy loins, and take my staff in thine hand, and go thy way: if thou meet any man, salute him not; and if any salute thee, answer him not again: and lay my staff upon the face of the child. And the mother of the child said, As the Lord liveth, and as thy soul liveth, I will not leave thee. And he arose, and followed her. And Gehazi passed on before them, and laid the staff upon the face of the child ; but there was neither voice, nor hearing. Wherefore he went again to meet him, and told him, saying, The child is not awaked. And when Elisha was come into the house, behold, the child was dead, and laid upon his bed. He went in therefore, and shut the door upon them twain, and prayed unto the Lord. And he went up, and lay upon the child, and put his mouth upon his mouth, and his eyes upon his eyes, and his hands upon his hands : and he stretched himself upon the child ; and the flesh of the child waxed warm. Then he returned, and walked in the house to and fro ; and went up, and stretched himself upon him : and the child sneezed seven times, and the child opened his eyes. And he called Gehazi, and said, Call this Shunammite. So he called her. And when she was come in unto him, he said, Take up thy son. Then she went in, and fell at his feet, and bowed herself to the ground, and took up her son, and went out."—2 Kings iv. 29—37.

Elisha had to deal with a dead child. It is true that, in his instance, it was natural death ; but the death with which you have to come in contact is not the less real death because it is spiritual. Boys and girls are as surely as grown-up people "dead in trespasses and sins." May none fail fully to realise the state in which all human beings are naturally found. Unless you have a very clear sense of the utter ruin and spiritual death of children, you will be incapable of being made a blessing to them. Go to them, I pray you, not as to sleepers whom you can by your own power awaken from their slumber, but as to spiritual corpses who can only be quickened by a power divine. Elisha aimed at nothing less than the restoration of the child to life. May you never be content with aiming at secondary benefits, or even with realising them; may you strive for the grandest of all ends, the salvation of immortal souls. Your business is not merely to teach children to read the Bible, not barely to inculcate the duties of morality, nor even to instruct them in the mere letter of the gospel, but your high calling is to be the means, in the hands of God, of bringing life from heaven to dead souls.

Resurrection, then, is our aim! To raise the dead is our mission! How is so strange a work to be achieved? If we yield to unbelief we shall be staggered by the evident fact that the work to which the Lord has called us is quite beyond our own personal power. We cannot raise the dead. We are, however, no more powerless than Elisha, for he of himself could not restore the Shunammite's son. Need this fact discourage us? Does it not rather direct us to our true power by shutting us out from our own fancied might? I trust we are all of us already aware that the man who lives in the region of faith dwells in the realm of miracles.

Elisha was no common man now that God's Spirit was upon him, calling him to God's work, and aiding him in it. And you, devoted, anxious, prayerful teacher, remain no longer a common being, you have become, in a special manner, the temple of the Holy Ghost; God dwelleth in you, and you by faith have entered upon the career of a wonder-worker. You are sent into the world not to do the things which are possible to man, but those impossibilities which God worketh by His Spirit,

by the means of His believing people. You are
to work miracles, to do marvels. You are not,
therefore, to look upon the restoration of these
dead children, which in God's name you are
called to bring about, as being a thing unlikely
or difficult when you remember who it is that
works by your feeble instrumentality.

It would have been well if Elisha had recollected
that he was once the servant of Elijah, and had so
studied his master's example as to have imitated
it. If so, he would not have sent Gehazi with a
staff, but have done at once what at last he was
constrained to do. In 1 Kings xvii. you will
find the story of Elijah raising a dead child, and
you will there see that Elijah, the master, had left
a complete example to his servant ; and it was not
till Elisha followed it in all respects that the
miraculous power was manifested. It had been
wise, I say, if Elisha had, at the outset, imitated
the example of the master whose mantle he wore.
With far more force may I say to you that it will
be well if, as teachers, we imitate the modes and
methods of our glorified Master, and learn at His
feet the art of winning souls. Just as He came in
deepest sympathy into the nearest contact with our
wretched humanity, and condescended to stoop to
our sorrowful condition, so must we come near to
the souls with whom we have to deal, yearn over
them with His yearning, and weep over them with
His tears, if we would see them raised from the
state of sin. Only by imitating the spirit and
manner of the Lord Jesus shall we become wise to

win souls. I am afraid that very often the truth which we deliver is a thing which is extraneous and out of ourselves ; like a staff which we hold in our hand, but which is not a part of ourselves. We take doctrinal or practical truth, as Gehazi did the staff, and we lay it upon the face of the child, but we ourselves do not agonise for its soul. We try this doctrine and that truth, this anecdote and the other illustration, this way of teaching a lesson and that manner of delivering an address ; but so long as ever the truth which we deliver is a matter apart from ourselves and unconnected with our innermost being, so long it will have no more effect upon a dead soul than Elisha's staff had upon the dead child. We are not sure that Gehazi was convinced that the child was really dead ; he spoke as if it were only asleep, and needed waking. God will not bless those teachers who do not grasp in their hearts the really fallen estate of their children. If you think the child is not really depraved, if you indulge foolish notions about the innocence of childhood and the dignity of human nature, it should not surprise you if you remain barren and unfruitful.

Observe carefully what Elisha did when thus foiled in his first effort. When we fail in one attempt, we must not therefore give up our work. If you have been unsuccessful until now, you must not infer that you are not called to the work, any more than Elisha might have concluded that the child could not be restored. The lesson of your non-success is not—cease the work, but—

change the method. It is not the person who is out of place, it is the plan which is unwise. If your first method has been unsuccessful, you must improve upon it. Examine wherein you have failed, and then, by changing your mode, or spirit, the Lord may prepare you for a degree of usefulness far beyond your expectation. Elisha, instead of being dispirited when he found that the child was not awake, girded up his loins, and hastened with greater vigour to the work before him.

THE SHUNAMMITE WOMAN'S
SON. II.

NOTICE where the dead child was placed: "And when Elisha was come into the house, behold, the child was dead, and laid upon his bed." This was the bed which the hospitality of the Shunammite had prepared for Elisha, the famous bed which, with the table, the stool, and the candlestick, will never be forgotten in the church of God.

In reading on we find "He went in, therefore, and shut the door upon them twain, and prayed unto the Lord." Now the prophet is at his work in right earnest, and we have a noble opportunity of learning from him the secret of raising children from the dead. If you turn to the narrative of Elijah, you will find that Elisha adopted the orthodox method of proceeding, the method of his master Elijah. You will read there, "And he said unto her, Give me thy son. And he took him out of her bosom, and carried him up into a loft, where he abode, and laid him upon his own bed. And he cried unto the Lord, and said, O Lord, my God, hast thou also brought evil upon the widow with whom I sojourn, by slaying her son? And he stretched himself upon the child three times, and cried unto the Lord, and said, O Lord, my God, I pray thee, let this child's soul come into him again. And the Lord heard the voice of Elijah ; and the soul of the child came into him again, and he revived." The great secret lies in a large measure in powerful supplication. " He shut the door upon them twain, and prayed unto the Lord." The old proverb is, " Every true pulpit is set up in heaven," by which is meant that the true preacher is much with God. If we do not pray to God for a blessing, if the foundation of the pulpit be not laid in private prayer, our open ministry will not be a success. So it is with you ; every real teacher's power must come from on high. If you never enter your closet and shut to the door, if you never plead at the mercy-seat for your child, how can you expect that God will honour you in its conversion? It is a very excellent method, I think, actually to take the children one by one into your room alone and pray with them. You will see your children converted when God gives you to individualise their cases, to agonize for them, and to take them one by one, and with the door closed to pray with them and for them. There is much with more influence in prayer privately offered with one than in prayer publicly uttered in the class—not more influence with God, of course, but more influence with the child. Such prayer will often be made its own answer ; for God may, while you are pouring out your soul, make your prayer to be a hammer to break the heart which mere addresses had never touched.

After praying, Elisha adopted the means. Prayer and means must go together. Means without prayer—presumption! Prayer without means —hypocrisy! There lay the child, and there stood the venerable man of God! Watch his singular proceeding; he stoops over the corpse and puts his mouth upon the child's mouth. The cold dead mouth of the child was touched by the warm living lips of the prophet, and a vital stream of fresh hot breath was sent down into the chill, stonelike passages of the dead mouth and throat and lungs. Next the holy man, with loving ardour of hopefulness, placed his eyes upon the child's eyes, and his hands upon the child's hands ; the warm hands of the old man covered the cold palms of the departed child. Then he stretched himself upon the child, and covered him with his whole body, as though he would transfer his own life into the lifeless frame, and would either die with him, or would make him live. We have heard of the chamois hunter acting as guide to a fearful traveller, who, when they came to a very dangerous part of the road, strapped the traveller firmly to himself, and said, " Both of us or neither," that is to say, " Both of us shall live, or neither of us, we are one." So did the prophet effect a mysterious union between himself and the lad, and in his own mind it was resolved that he would either be chilled with the child's death, or warm the child with his life.

What does this teach us? The lessons are many
and obvious. We see here, as in a picture, that if
we would bring spiritual life to a child, we must
most vividly realise that child's state. It is dead,
dead. God will have you feel that the child is as
dead in trespasses and sins as you once were. God
would have you come into contact with that death
by painful, crushing, humbling sympathy. In
soul-winning, we should observe how our Master
worked ; now how did He work? When He would
raise us from death, what did it behove Him to do?
He must needs die himself : there was no other way.
So it is with you. If you would raise that dead child,
you must feel the chill and horror of that child's
death yourself. A dying man is needed to raise
dying men. I cannot believe that you will ever
pluck a brand from the burning, without putting
your hand near enough to feel the heat of the fire.
You must have, more or less, a distinct sense of
the dreadful wrath of God and of the terrors of
the judgment to come, or you will lack energy in
your work, and so lack one of the essentials of
success. I do not think the preacher ever speaks
well upon such topics until he feels them pressing
upon him as a personal burden from the Lord.
" I did preach in chains," said John Bunyan, "to
men in chains." Depend upon it, when the death
that is in your children alarms, depresses, and
overwhelms you, then it is that God is about to
bless you. Thus realising the child's state, and
putting your mouth upon the child's mouth, and
your hands upon its hands, you must next strive

to adapt yourself as far as possible to the nature, and habits, and temperament of the child. Your mouth must find out the child's words, so that the child may know what you mean ; you must see things with a child's eyes ; your heart must feel a child's feelings, so as to be his companion and friend ; you must be a student of juvenile sin ; you must be a sympathiser in juvenile trials ; you must, so far as possible, enter into childhood's joys and griefs. You must not fret at the difficulty of this matter, or feel it to be humiliating. If anything difficult be required, you must do it, and not think it difficult. God will not raise a dead child by you if you are not willing to become all things to that child, if by any possibility you may win its soul.

The prophet, "*stretched himself upon the child.*" One would have thought it should be written " he contracted himself !" He was a full-grown man, and the other a mere lad. Should it not be " he contracted himself " ? No, " he stretched himself ; " and, mark you, no stretching is harder than for a man to stretch himself to a child. He is no fool who can talk to children ; a simpleton is much mistaken if he thinks that his folly can interest boys and girls. It needs our best wits, our most industrious studies, our most earnest thoughts, our ripest powers, to teach our little ones. You will not quicken the child until you have " stretched " yourself ; and, though it seems a strange thing, yet it is so. The wisest man will need to exercise all his abilities if he would become a successful teacher of the young.

We see, then, in Elisha, a sense of the child's
death and an adaptation of himself to his work,
but above all, we see *sympathy*. While Elisha
himself felt the chill of the corpse, his personal
warmth was entering into the dead body. This of
itself did not raise the child ; but God worked
through it—the old man's heat of body passed into
the child, and became the medium of quickening.
Let every teacher weigh these words of Paul, " But
we were gentle among you, even as a nurse cherish-
eth her children : so being affectionately desirous
of you, we were willing to have imparted unto
you, not the gospel of God only, *but also our
own souls*, because ye were dear unto us." God
will bless by His Spirit our hearty sympathy
with His own truth, and make it do that which the
truth alone coldly spoken would not accomplish.
Here, then, is the secret. You must impart to the
young your own soul ; you must feel as if the ruin
of that child would be your own ruin.

The result of the prophet's work soon appeared,
" The flesh of the child waxed warm." How
pleased Elisha must have been ; but I do not find
that his pleasure and satisfaction caused him to
relax his exertions. Never be satisfied with finding
your children in a barely hopeful state. What you
want is not mere conviction, but conversion ; you
desire not only impression, but regeneration. Life,
life from God, the life of Jesus. This your scholars
need, and nothing less must content you.

"*Then he returned, and walked in the house to and
fro.*" Notice the restlessness of the man of God ;

he cannot be easy. The child waxes warm (blessed be God for that), but he does not live yet ; so, instead of sitting down by the table, the prophet walks to and fro with restless foot, disquieted, groaning, panting, longing, and ill at ease. He could not bear to look upon the disconsolate mother, or to hear her ask, " Is the child restored?" but he continued pacing the house as if his body could not rest because his soul was not satisfied. Imitate this consecrated restlessness. When you see a boy getting somewhat affected, do not sit down and say, " The child is very hopeful, thank God ; I am perfectly satisfied." You will never win the priceless gem of a saved soul in that way ; you must feel sad, restless, troubled, if you ever become a parent in the church.

After a short period of walking to and fro, the prophet again "went up and stretched himself upon the child." What it is well to do once, it is proper to do a second time. What is good twice, is good seven times. There must be perseverance and patience. As surely as warmth went from Elisha to the child, so may cold go from you to your class unless you are in an earnest state of mind.

Elisha stretched himself on the bed again with many a prayer, and many a sigh, and much believing, and at last his desire was granted him. " *The child sneezed seven times, and the child opened his eyes.*" Any form of action would indicate life, and content the prophet. The child "sneezed," some say, because he died with a disease of the head, for he said to his father, " My head ! my head !" and the sneeze cleared the passages of life which had been blocked up. This we do not know. The fresh air entering afresh into the lungs might well compel a sneeze. The sound was nothing very articulate or musical, but it betokened life. This is all we should expect from young children when God gives them spiritual life. Some church members expect a great deal more, but for my part I am satisfied if the children sneeze—if they give any true sign of grace, however feeble or indistinct.

Perhaps if Gehazi had been there he would not have thought much of this sneezing, because he had never stretched himself upon the child, but Elisha was content with it. Even so, if you and I have really agonised in prayer for souls, we shall be very quick of eye to catch the first sign of grace, and shall be thankful to God if the token be but a sneeze.

Then the child *opened its eyes,* and we will venture to say Elisha thought he had never seen such lovely eyes before. I know not what kind of eyes they were, the hazel or the blue, but this I know, that any eye which God helps you to open will be a beautiful eye to you.